THE GARDEN AVIARY

GAIL HARLAND

AMBERLEY

For Ash and Jonny

First published 2023

Amberley Publishing
The Hill, Stroud,
Gloucestershire, GL5 4EP

www.amberley-books.com

Copyright © Gail Harland, 2023

The right of Gail Harland to be identified as the Author
of this work has been asserted in accordance with the
Copyrights, Designs and Patents Act 1988.

ISBN: 978 1 3981 1319 0 (print)
ISBN: 978 1 3981 1320 6 (ebook)

British Library Cataloguing in Publication Data.
A catalogue record for this book is available from the British Library.

Typeset in 9.5pt on 11pt Celeste.
Typesetting by SJmagic DESIGN SERVICES, India.
Printed in the UK.

Contents

The Attraction of Birds

The beauty of birds

Birds have been admired and envied, hunted and eaten for thousands of years. More than seventy species of birds have been identified in ancient Egyptian art, but some bird images predate even those. The Lascaux Palaeolithic cave paintings in France, estimated to be up to 20,000 years old, include intriguing images of a bird on a stick and a human-bird hybrid. Flocks of birds are pictured in Spanish Neolithic cave art at the Cueva del Tajo de las Figuras (Cave of the Figures on the Precipice) at Benalup-Casas Viejas in the province of Cádiz. Images there include some that look like the northern bald ibis (*Geronticus eremita*), which has been the subject of a recent reintroduction programme in southern Spain. At the base of a mineshaft at the ancient Grimes Graves flint mines near Thetford in Norfolk, the skull of a phalarope, a type of wading bird, was found flanked by a pair of antler picks and a Cornish stone axe. It would presumably have had some cultural significance to the workers there around 2500 BC.

The northern bald ibis is one of the most endangered bird species worldwide. It became extinct in Central Europe in the seventeenth century due to hunting pressure.

Some British henges and circles of the Neolithic period contain deposits of pottery and animal and bird bones in their ditches. The birds are mostly ravens and crows and have been interpreted as offerings to the earth. Of course we have no way of knowing if the raven bones unearthed were from wild birds freshly caught and killed or perhaps from hand-reared birds taken from the nest, reared as companions and mourned when they died. Ravens normally live for between twenty and twenty-five years; one tame bird at the Tower of London even reached forty-four years of age. At Danebury Iron Age hill fort in Hampshire, some of the skeletons found were certainly of long-lived birds, so it is possible that some birds buried in pits may have been companion animals or familiars to religious elders. The character and behaviour of ravens and crows gave them significance in later prehistoric and classical times. Both species are scavengers and would have lived alongside human settlements, which may have given them a role in the Iron Age as agents in sky burials and the rite of excarnation. In Roman times their voice and calls led to the belief that they communicated with the gods.

Julius Caesar believed that Britons considered it wrong 'to partake of hare, cockerel, or geese, but they keep these instead for reasons of affection and pleasure.' Britons certainly have a long and ongoing history of keeping all manner of birds for their beauty and companionship. The beauty of birds and our fascination with them is indisputable. The Royal Society for the Protection of Birds is the UK's largest nature conservation charity and in 2021 over one million people took part in their Big Garden Birdwatch. Some of our native birds have an obvious jewel-like beauty; just think of the iridescent blue and orange plumage of a kingfisher or the male bullfinch's black cap contrasting with his rose-pink breast. Even the less showy species can enthral us with the diversity of their feathers and forms and the fascination of their behaviours and individual characters. And of course, we envy birds their ability to fly and the freedom that gives them.

Beauty is not just in the eye of the beholder but also in the ear and many birds are more renowned for their calls and songs than their appearance. Music was of great importance in classical Greek culture. In Homer's *Odyssey* the singing nightingale is compared to a woman grieving for her lost child. Nightingales were popular cage birds in Roman times

American artist Jonathan Eastman Johnson (1824–1906) was known for his paintings of scenes from everyday life. *The Pets* (1856) shows a young girl whose kitten is showing great interest in the bowl of goldfish while her Amazon parrot looks on. (The National Gallery of Art, Washington DC)

Andean geese usually mix well with other birds, but during the breeding season can become aggressive and need a separate aviary.

The bullfinch combines good looks with a surprising ability as a mimic. It was widely kept as a cage bird in Victorian times as it would imitate sounds such as a flute or whistle.

and Pliny discussed the high prices that the best singers could achieve. The canary was first kept as a cage bird in Europe in the late 1400s and soon became more popular than the nightingale because it is easier to rear in captivity and sings not just in the springtime but for much of the year. Selective breeding of canaries, particularly in Germany, focused on producing birds with the best songs. These became known as roller canaries because of their rolling song.

The German Baron von Pernau (1660–1731), a wealthy politician, was interested in birds and his observations of both wild and captive birds demonstrated that the song is not instinctive but the result of learning. The English lawyer and naturalist Daines Barrington (1727–1800) conducted one of the first scientific studies of birdsong. He asked surgeon John Hunter to dissect some birds and to examine their vocal cords. They found that species such as nightingales with more complex songs had stronger muscles in the larynx, particularly in male birds.

Recent research has found that those sexual differences in the larynx are reflected in the brain. The region of a bird's brain responsible for song, known as the higher vocal centre (HVC), is up to four times bigger in males than in females. Because song-learning requires considerable

Aviary with Fourteen Birds, an eighteenth-century artwork, possibly by the Dutch painter and glass engraver Aert Schouman. (Rijksmuseum, Amsterdam)

brain power, the HVC is bigger in those species that sing more complex songs. Female birds have a smaller HVC because processing male song and deciding who sings better is less demanding than actually producing the song, inviting interesting comparisons with human talent show contestants and judges.

The wild bird caged

Keeping songbirds is still a very popular hobby in places such as Cuba and in Singapore where bird-singing pageants and competitions bring an important social aspect to the activity, but bird cages for keeping live birds have been known since written records began. The Sumerians of the late Neolithic period used the word subura for birdcage. The ancient Egyptians kept birds on ornamental ponds at their homes and reared birds such as ibis specifically to be mummified in their funeral rites. The ibis was sacred to the scribe god Thoth and the penalty for killing a wild one was death. In Buddhist, Jain and Hindu art of the early historic period (sixth–third century BC) there are many representations of the mythological figures yakshas and the female counterpart, the yakshi. They may have represented the spirits that inhabited natural elements such as trees, mountains, rivers, and the oceans. Their prevalence in Asian sculpture is considered a sign of widespread nature worship. The Bhutesvara yakshis are a series of stone reliefs around the remains of a Buddhist stupa, outside Mathura in the Indian state of Uttar Pradesh. They date to the time of the Kushan Empire and depict voluptuous females wearing only diaphanous skirts. One of the yakshis has a pet parrot perched on her shoulder and holds its cage in her hand. In other examples a parrot nibbles at food offered by the yakshi. A similar yakshi holding a child and accompanied by a parrot is held at the Metropolitan Museum of Art in New York.

Above: Dutch artist Jan Steen painted a scene including the family macaw and caged songbirds to illustrate the proverb 'As the old sing, so pipe the young' (1665), The Mauritshuis, The Hague, the Netherlands.

Left: Yakshi stonework from first-century India. (The Metropolitan Museum of Art, New York)

In the Americas, brightly coloured birds such as the scarlet macaw were highly prized for their feathers and had cultural and cosmological associations. Excavations at Paquime in modern-day Chihuahua, Mexico, have found fifty-six mudbrick enclosures with nest boxes and the remains of over 500 macaws, indicating an active breeding programme taking place in the community between 1150 and 1450 AD. When in 1521 the Spanish conquistador Hernán Cortés entered Tenochtitlan, the capital of the Aztec empire, the Spanish were very impressed with the garden of beasts and birds there. As described by Bernal Diaz,

> Every kind of bird that was there and its peculiarity, for there was everything from the Royal Eagle and other smaller eagles, and many other birds of great size, down to tiny birds of many-coloured plumage, also birds from which they take the rich plumage which they use in their green feather work. The birds which have these feathers are about the size of the magpies in Spain, they are called in this country Quezales, and there are other birds which have feathers of five colours—green, red, white, yellow and blue... All the birds that I have spoken about breed in these houses, and in the setting season certain Indian men and women who look after the birds, place the eggs under them and clean the nests and feed them, so that each kind of bird has its proper food.

Birds have even been used as navigational aids. Seafarers including the Babylonians and Vikings carried caged birds on long ocean journeys. Like the biblical Noah with his raven and dove, when seeking land they would release the bird. If the bird could see land, it would fly in that direction but if there were no land in sight, the bird would return to the ship. Birds continued to be appreciated on board ship, even in the days of radar. An article on naval pets in the 1 July 1911 issue of *The Sphere* discussed how British navy men kept their caged pet canaries on board the HMS *Illustrious*.

Caged birds figure commonly in early European art from medieval bestiaries to religious icons. The goldfinch is a common bird in Europe and during the Renaissance period it was a favourite household pet, often kept tied to a long string or chain. The birds were taught to perform tricks such as ringing a bell or drawing up water using a tiny bucket on a chain. The red feathers on its face were said to have arisen when the goldfinch tried to remove a thorn from Christ's crown during the crucifixion, and was stained with a drop of blood. Thus, the

This stirrup-spout vessel in the shape of a parrot was produced by Moche artists of Peru's north coast (350–550 AD). (The Metropolitan Museum of Art, New York)

Abraham Mignon's *Fruit Still-Life with Squirrel and Goldfinch* (*c.* 1668) shows the goldfinch drawing up a thimbleful of water from the suspended glass. (Museumslandschaft Hessen, Kassel, Germany)

Above left: Parrots feature in very early religious works such as *The Madonna and Child with the Parrot* by Martin Schongauer, 1470, where it is thought to represent the Virgin birth of Christ. (The Metropolitan Museum of Art, New York)

Above right: *The Virgin and Child with the Parrot* by Hans Sebald Beham from Nuremberg in Germany (1549).

Above left: François Boucher's *The Bird Catchers* (1748) is one of the most famous paintings of the Rococo period with its pastoral scene of young lovers playing with birds. (J. Paul Getty Museum)

Above right: Many bird cages, such as this beautiful example made from Delft pottery, were more ornamental than functional.

bird is used extensively in religious painting by artists such as Raphael. The French Rococo artist François Boucher's famous painting *The Bird Catchers* (1748) shows a group of young fashionable couples playing with caged birds, holding them on their fingers or tethered on strings. At the time if a man gave a caged bird to his amour, it signified that she had captured his heart. The cages, as was common at the time, were very small with no concern for bird welfare.

Serving their country; the messenger pigeon and the coal miner's canary

Today the mobile phone is very much the communication device of choice but in earlier times people relied on pigeons. Pigeons can fly at around 60 miles per hour and manage distances of between 600 and 700 miles in a single day. Cyrus the Great, king of the Persian Empire in the sixth century BC, used carrier pigeons to communicate across his territories, and in ancient Rome Julius Caesar employed pigeons to send messages to Gaul. Pigeons were highly regarded for their use in wartime. During the Franco-Prussian War of 1870–71, besieged Parisians relied on the birds to transmit messages outside the city. The pigeons could carry microfilm images containing hundreds of messages from as far away as London. The Prussian army tried to counteract these feathered messengers by employing hawks to hunt them down.

Extensive use of homing pigeons occurred during the First World War. In 1914, during the First Battle of the Marne, the French army advanced seventy-two pigeon lofts along with the troops. The Dickin Medal was inaugurated in 1943 by Maria Dickin, the founder of the People's Dispensary for Sick Animals (PDSA), to honour the work of animals in the Second World War. Of fifty-four Dickin Medals awarded between 1943 and 1949, thirty-two went to pigeons. One, a pigeon named Mary of Exeter, owned by bootmaker Charlie Brewer, served with the National Pigeon Service and made four trips from France back to her loft in Exeter between 1940 and 1945. She was awarded

LES PIGEONS VOYAGEURS DE LA MARINE BRITANNIQUE

Officier d'un sous-marin britannique envoyant une dépêche par pigeon voyageur

Wartime messenger pigeon photographed for this French postcard.

the Dickin Medal in November 1945 for endurance on war service despite being injured on three occasions. She died in 1950 and is buried at the animal cemetery in Ilford, London. Another Dickin Medal winner was a pigeon known as Royal Blue who was owned by Queen Elizabeth II.

Carrier pigeons were used for emergency communication right up to the twenty-first century by remote police departments in eastern India. The Police Pigeon Service in Orissa ceased in March 2002 due to the expanded use of the internet. The visual navigational skills of pigeons enable them to be used as medical imaging data sorters. Under research conditions, they can be trained to examine data on a screen for the purposes of detecting breast cancer. The United States Coast Guard search and rescue division has shown that pigeons are significantly better than humans at spotting orange life jackets in water.

Other bird species can save lives too. The idea of using canaries down mines originated with John Scott Haldane (1860–1936), an Edinburgh physician famous for testing poisonous gases on himself. Haldane visited the scenes of many mining disasters to investigate their causes. He concluded that an explosion at Tylorstown Colliery in 1896 resulted from a build-up of carbon monoxide. His research led him to recommend using animals with a fast metabolism such as white mice or canaries to detect dangerous levels of carbon monoxide underground. Birds are the best choice as their lungs hold air in extra sacs, receiving a dose of oxygen when they inhale and another when they exhale, so they get twice as much air and therefore poisonous gases as do mice. Birds show the effects of poisoning before gas levels become critical for humans, and so were an effective early warning system.

Under the 1911 Coal Mines Act a minimum of two canaries had to be kept at a coal mine by law but it was usual practice to keep more than this. The birds were not just another piece of equipment, but were valued team members and the miners would often whistle to them and treat them as pets. Special cages were made to try to resuscitate birds after gas exposure. Canary use in British pits started to be replaced by electronic gas detectors in 1986, and in 1996 the use of canaries in British collieries came to an end. They were replaced by a handheld carbon-monoxide detector, known as the 'Electronic Canary', but many pits kept an aviary of canaries near the colliery manager's office as a tradition, in recognition of the many lives saved.

Companion animals that can talk back

The earliest reference to a talking bird comes from Ctesias of Cnidus and dates to the late fifth century BC when he was working as a court physician in Persia. The bird, known as Bittacus, was probably a plum-headed parakeet imported from India and was described as 'about as large as a hawk, which has a human tongue and voice, a dark red beak, a black beard, and blue feathers up to the neck, which is red like cinnabar. It speaks Indian like a native, and if taught Greek, speaks Greek.' The barber-surgeon on board the ship *The Amsterdam*, during the second Dutch expedition to the East Indies in search of spices, purchased a red and yellow parrot that could crow like a cock, mimic the cat and spoke several words. The German naturalist Alexander von Humboldt (1769–1859) when travelling in South America encountered a parrot that was the last living repository of the language of the extinct Atures Indian tribe. Wild cockatoos in Australia have been reported to have learned human speech from ex-captive birds that have integrated into the flock.

Many birds have a degree of talking ability. Corvids are able to mimic a few words and phrases, while the hill mynah and its relative the European starling are well known for mimicry. The talking ability of the budgerigar was first described in the 1780s when Thomas Watling trained his bird to greet his employer with the words 'How do you do Dr White?' Many pet budgerigars can repeat a large number of words and phrases. The Guinness World Record for the most extensive bird vocabulary was held by a budgerigar named Puck, owned by Camille Jordan of California, who had learnt 1,728 words by the time of his death in 1994.

Old Lady (about to purchase parrot)
" Does it swear."

Old Salt : " Not so bad for sich a young bird,"

Above left: Comic postcard, pre-1921. Sailors' parrots were notorious for swearing.

Above right: The yellow-thighed caique (*Pionites xanthomerius*) is a South American species of parrot.

Above left: The rose-breasted cockatoo (*Eolophus roseicapilla*), commonly known as the galah is found throughout Australia and has been introduced to Tasmania.

Above right: A red-tailed black cockatoo (*Calyptorhynchus banksii*) enjoying the sunshine.

Left: The verse on this engraving *The Parrot* by French artist Abraham Bosse (1622) refers to the parrot speaking with a human tongue. (The Metropolitan Museum of Art, New York)

Jamais oiseau dans vn boccage,
En chantant ne fit tant de bruit,
Qu'en fait celui-cy dans sa cage,
De la façon quil est instruit.

Ame cajolle il me caresse,
Imitant le langage inumain,
Mesme il m'appelle sa maistresse,
Et s'en vient manger sur ma main.

Mais ô que je serois heureuse,
Si ie pouuois par mon caquet.
Flatter mon inimeur amoureuse,
Aussi bien que ce Perroquet.

African grey parrots are highly intelligent birds and excellent mimics.

Most of the best talking birds are members of the parrot family. There is debate within the scientific community over whether they are merely repeating familiar sounds or if they have some understanding of the language. Irene Pepperberg is well known for her studies of the African grey parrot. The main focus of her work is the cognitive and communicative abilities of the species and to compare their abilities with those of great apes, marine mammals, and young children. Her most famous study bird, Alex, was with her for thirty years until his death in 2007, and he learned over 100 English words and fifty object names. He could identify colours, shapes, and quantities and ask questions, including asking what colour he was, which indicates a degree of self-awareness.

People and their pets

Many famous people have had pet birds. Henry VIII owned an African grey parrot which could cause havoc by imitating the whistle used to call ferry men across the River Thames. During the reign of the Queen Elizabeth I, exploration of Central and South America ensured a supply of colourful Amazon parrots that became very popular in the royal court. Elizabeth herself was presented with a parrot in 1596 by Sir John Gilbert of Compton Castle. He gave the Queen detailed instructions on the care of her new pet, advising that the bird should be kept warm and not given salty foods. It should be put on the table at mealtimes and be allowed to select his own foods and that 'after he hath filled himself he will sit in a gentlewoman's ruff all the day.'

Queen Victoria was given a parrot by her Uncle Ernest when she was a seventeen-year-old princess. She described it in her journal as, 'a most delightful Lory which is so tame that it remains on your hand and you may put your finger into its beak or do anything with it without its ever attempting to bite.' The lory later featured with a spaniel, deerhound and greyhound in a painting by Landseer titled *Queen Victoria's Favourite Pets*.

Minna, the first wife of the German composer Richard Wagner, had a parrot named Papo that she had trained to say, whenever Richard raised his voice, 'Bad man! Poor Minna.' The parrot whistled themes from Beethoven's symphonies and could greet friends of the couple individually by name. If Wagner left the sitting room for any length of time the parrot would

Above left: *A Woman Feeding a Parrot with her Page*, by Dutch portrait painter Caspar Netscher (1666). (The National Gallery of Art, Washington DC)

Above right: African grey parrot appears as a young woman's confidant in Edouard Manet's painting *Young Lady in 1866*. The model, Victorine Meurent, had posed for his better-known paintings *Olympia* and *Luncheon on the Grass* (both at the Musée d'Orsay, Paris). (The Metropolitan Museum of Art, New York)

Left: Colourful birds such as this Barraband's parrakeet from south-eastern Australia are popular pets.

repeatedly call out 'Richard', and then flutter into the study to look for him. Papo died in 1851 and was greatly mourned by Wagner.

Polly has been the most popular name for English pet parrots since the time of Ben Jonson's comic work *Volpone* in 1605. The English composer Sir Arthur Sullivan, known for works such as *HMS Pinafore*, had a parrot called Polly whose catchphrase was 'Polly, what's the time?' Sullivan's colleague, the librettist W.S. Gilbert was even more of a bird-fancier. He had a large estate at Harrow Weald where he built an ornate pigeon house for his fantail pigeons. His own parrot had a cage in the entrance hall of the house. It was reputed to be the finest talking parrot in England and could whistle the hornpipe. Gilbert sometimes looked after his friend's parrot and joked that his parrot took in pupils for tuition in talking.

Samuel Pepys recorded in his diary in 1660 the purchase of two cages for the canaries sent to him by Captain Rooth but surprisingly, when the musical genius Wolfgang Amadeus Mozart bought himself a bird, it was not a canary but a pet starling. He noted the event in his expense book, recording the price paid and a transcription of the song the bird sang with the comment 'Das war schon' (that was beautiful). This fragment of song is the same as the theme from the last movement of Mozart's Piano Concerto in G major, causing scholars to speculate on whether Mozart copied the sound from his bird or the bird had learned to mimic the theme. The short piece known as 'A Musical Joke', written by Mozart just eight days after his pet died, is thought to be based on the starling's song. Mozart had had his starling for three years when it died and buried it with great ceremony. Mourners were invited to join in a procession and to sing hymns and listen to a poem that Mozart had written for the occasion.

English travellers have always brought back ideas as well as souvenirs from their foreign travels. Visitors to the Chateau de Seneffe in France can see the beautiful aviaries and a decidedly quirky nesting box.

Above: The aviary at Chateau de Seneffe is used for whistling tree ducks.

Left: Close-up of the communal nesting box at Chateau de Seneffe.

Snowy owl (*Bubo scandiacus*) at Tropical Birdland, Desford.

Birds featuring in children's literature can spark an enthusiasm for pet birds among young readers. Green talking parrots are important characters in Robert Louis Stevenson's book *Treasure Island* and in Arthur Ransome's popular *Swallows and Amazons* series in the 1930s and 1940s. At the end of the 1990s the huge interest in the Harry Potter books written by J.K. Rowling, featuring a snowy owl called Hedwig, led to fears that children would be demanding pet owls then abandoning them when the fad subsided. Researchers however found that this was not the case and fortunately the end of the Harry Potter film series did not result in an increase of unwanted pet owls turning up at wildlife sanctuaries.

Concepts of Freedom

Parrots were often tethered to a stand by one foot so they could stretch their wings but not fly away, as pictured on this 'oilette' postcard by Raphael Tuck, dating from around 1906. An oilette was a type of postcard with the surface designed to appear as a miniature oil painting.

Cages, aviaries and free flight

Originally written and recorded in 1977 by John Lennon, although not released as a single until 1995, the Beatles song 'Free as a Bird' combines thoughts of freedom with those of home. For some people freedom and home are incompatible concepts and there are no shades of grey; a caged bird is always an abomination, reminding them of William Blake's words in *Auguries of Innocence*, 'A Robin Red breast in a Cage, Puts all Heaven in a Rage.' The very word 'cage' can be highly emotive, suggesting prison in a way that the chicken's coop or a dog's basket does not. However if you open the door of a pet budgie's cage, it will usually choose to come out, spread its wings and explore the sitting room, getting enjoyment from perching on the window pole or poking around the book shelves, but most will then take themselves back to their cage to feed and to roost safely at night. It could be argued that equating a caged bird with a human prisoner behind bars is anthropomorphising the bird, and that for pet birds their cage is a sanctuary – their home, not a prison.

Right: Birds behind bars often look forlorn to the viewer, as the tendency is to ascribe them human emotions, but this cockatiel could also be described as contemplative, pensive or relaxed.

Below: Providing inspiration for the would-be aviary owner in 1928, the Ideal Home Exhibition included a *Daily Mail*-sponsored garden with a small ornamental aviary surrounded by crazy paving and rockwork.

AN AVIARY GARDEN. "DAILY MAIL" IDEAL HOME EXHIBITION. 1928. No.18.

During the pandemic lockdowns when human freedom of movement was curtailed, many people found solace in the natural world. A survey commissioned by the Royal Society for the Protection of Birds reported that over half of UK adults said the pandemic has made them more aware of nature in their local area. Many people watching the birds may have envied them their freedom to fly. However Aldous Huxley argued that flight to a bird may just be a drain on its resources.

The proportion of existing bird species that are flightless is comparatively small, with only sixty flightless bird species surviving today. They tend to be inhabitants of islands without mammal predators or large birds such as the ostrich, which excels in outrunning predators, and the cassowary whose formidable clawed toes can inflict fatal wounds. However, flightlessness evolved much more frequently among birds than may be expected. Swedish researchers compiled a list of all bird species known to have gone extinct since the rise of humans. They found that fossil records show 166 out of 581 extinct species identified lacked the ability to fly. Flightless birds were much more diverse than previous studies had assumed but also much more likely to go extinct than species that could fly. This was due to in part to hunting by humans but also predation by introduced rats and cats, such as Tiddles the cat of David Lyall, a lighthouse keeper on New Zealand's Stephens Island, which hastened the extinction of a previously unrecognised flightless wren.

During the pandemic pet owners reported that having birds and other animals meant they were less lonely, as well as giving them a sense of purpose. When taking on care of a bird, that sense of purpose must come with a sense of responsibility and the bird's welfare has to be paramount. Choices have to be made between cage, aviary or allowing at least some degree of free flight. While caring for a budgerigar called Diogenes, Nicholas Lezard wrote in the *New Statesman*, 'What's so bad about a cage? It's just like a home, or a good marriage, and there's nothing axiomatically wrong about either of those things.' However most people agree that the greater space and the potential for planting and a more varied habitat in an aviary is better for a bird's physical and mental wellbeing. Many birds, like humans, synthesise vitamin D when exposed to the sun's ultraviolet rays, so if not kept in an outdoor aviary with exposure to sunshine, they may require full spectrum bird lighting or vitamin D supplementation.

The Victoria crowned pigeon (*Goura victoria*) is the largest living pigeon. Native to the New Guinea region, it was named in honour of Queen Victoria. It can fly short distances but prefers to forage on the floor, only flying to roost in the trees at night.

Above: Well-built aviaries at Lotherton Hall in Leeds.

Right: This plucked blue and gold macaw is now part of a mixed flock of parrots with freedom to fly and exhibit natural behaviours.

There is no standard definition as to when a cage becomes an aviary and ideas about suitability of structures have changed over time. The raven cage designed by Decimus Burton at London Zoo is regarded as one of their oldest structures. It was built in 1829 and was originally created as summer accommodation for the zoo's macaws, but visitors today would be appalled to see such big birds confined there and it is no longer considered suitable to use. In 1965 the zoo became home to Britain's first walk-through aviary. Created as a collaboration between Antony Armstrong-Jones, 1st Earl of Snowdon, with architect Cedric Price and structural engineer Frank Newby, the Grade II listed Snowdon Aviary was pioneering in its use of aluminium and tension for support. Originally home to forty-five different species including Hartlaub's turacos, alpine chough, sacred ibis and Von der Decken's hornbills, over time it fell into disrepair and it was recreated and renamed Monkey Valley in 2022, providing a new home for the zoo's troop of ten Eastern black-and-white colobus monkeys and a colony of African grey parrots.

Blue and gold macaws at Tropical Birdland, Desford.

Sewerby Hall and Gardens in Yorkshire is known for its work with the World Pheasant Association and their breeding of the critically endangered Edward's pheasants in association with the European Endangered Breeding Programme. Their new walk-through aviary is an attractive construction for water birds including the rosy-billed pochard, with black nylon mesh at the top and a weld mesh at the bottom. An electric fence around the perimeter is active at night to ensure the structure is fox proof.

Education is an important role for zoological and other collections.

The waterfowl aviary at Sewerby Hall near Bridlington will allow visitors to walk through when bird flu restrictions are not in operation. It is home to fourteen different species including mandarin duck, white-faced whistling duck and the New Zealand shoveler.

The pheasant pens at Sewerby Hall include species such as the Edwards pheasant (*Lophura edwardsi*) from Vietnam and play an important contribution to the European endangered breeding programme.

Birds of Eden bird sanctuary, located in the Western Cape of South Africa, is one of the largest free flight aviaries in the world. The aviary opened in 2005 and covers an area of 2.3 hectares (5.7 acres). The mesh-domed aviary spans over a gorge of indigenous forest and includes a waterfall and a 200-seat amphitheatre. It is home to around 3,000 individual birds from 200 species. The emphasis is on native African species but inhabitants include some rehomed, previously caged pets such as macaws and other parrots. Before any new birds are released into the sanctuary, they undergo rehabilitation to improve their flying ability.

An aviary, however large, is still a place of confinement and many people have experimented with free flying their non-native birds. The late Queen Elizabeth II was given two budgies as a gift in the 1930s. They were of a strain known as Liberty budgerigars which are close to the wild species rather than being highly bred exhibition birds. These were the start of a flock of around 100 birds that were kept in an aviary at Windsor Castle and allowed freedom to come and go from their aviary through a wire mesh access tube. The keeper of the royal budgerigars, Graham Stone, reported that the Queen was very fond of the birds but they had had some problems with bird fertility due to inbreeding.

African greys benefit from the company of their own kind as here in an aviary at Tropical Birdland, Desford.

Hastings Russell, the 12th Duke of Bedford, who lived for about ten years at the Woburn Abbey estate in Bedfordshire, was a noted keeper and breeder of birds. He was author of *Parrots and Parrot-like Birds* and regularly published articles in the avicultural press. A complicated man, described by his eldest son as 'The loneliest man I ever knew, incapable of giving or receiving love, utterly self-centred and opinionated. He loved birds, animals, peace, monetary reform, the park and religion.' The Duke was an advocate of homing budgerigars and allowed his birds to free fly for periods of liberty which he felt toned them up before the breeding season. In 1952 he wrote, 'It is not easy to see on what principle hen Budgerigars select their mates. They certainly do not always choose the bravest and strongest, as do hen grouse, and they certainly do not always choose the most beautiful; in fact, they display such a shocking disregard of the standards of the Budgerigar Society that I have often thought of adorning the side of the hen's aviary with the drawing of the Ideal Cock Budgerigar as a sort of pin-up boy.' When the Duke died in 1953, an aviary for homing budgerigars was erected in his memory at London Zoo. They had to be confined to the aviary after a few years because sparrowhawks and other predators were catching them while they were flying in Regent's Park.

It is not just sparrowhawks that have to be considered. In bad weather or if frightened, birds may be disorientated and not be able to find their way back. Many birds have a high monetary value, which inevitably means they may be a target for thieves and sadly, not everyone loves birds. A parrot breeder in Essex allowed a pair of bonded African greys to free fly but found that both birds were shot by a farmer.

Training birds to allow them to fly outdoors without restraint and then return to their handler can be successful in some situations with positive benefits to the birds' wellbeing. Free flying parrots are less likely to pluck their own feathers or suffer respiratory problems than those confined to a cage. Positive reinforcement training is important to ensure that they want to return. Many birds show strong roosting site fidelity and do not want to fly far from their flock, food supply and the emotional security of home. Motley, a harlequin macaw owned by zoo biology student Chloe Brown, became a social media star after images of him free flying around the Peak District went viral. Brown believes the benefits it provides her parrot, including mental stimulation and exercise, outweigh the risks. 'His absolute favourite place is Curbar Edge in the peaks. The thermals come straight up the cliff and he just loves it.'

Above left: Feather plucking can be a sign of disease but also occurs in parrots that have been stressed or bored.

Above right: A healthy African grey parrot exhibiting normal preening behaviour.

Right: Native to the forests of Mexico and South America, military macaws are social birds and prefer to live in flocks.

Tropical Birdland at Desford in Leicestershire is home to over 250 birds from around the world. Many of the parrots are allowed to fly outdoors during the day and enjoy engaging with visitors. Some of the young visitors have never experienced such close interaction with birds before and are delighted to find that such colourful creatures may consider their head or shoulder to be a suitable perch.

In the days before animal welfare issues were widely considered, birds were often used as performing animals in circuses and other shows. Widely known as the Bird

The mixed species free-flight parrots at Tropical Birdland, Desford, enjoy one another's company.

Collections with free-living birds allow children to have close encounters with species they may otherwise never see, as here while sharing lunch with a Moluccan cockatoo.

Man of Llandudno, Italian-born Gicianto Ferrari (1847–1923) moved to Britain as a child, initially training as a baker. He developed a performing bird show using trained canaries, budgerigars and caiques. Despite squabbles with rival street entertainer the Punch and Judy man Richard Codman, the show became very popular with visitors to Llandudno, including the war poet Wilfred Owen. One of his more controversial tricks was firing a gun while three of his birds perched unperturbed on the barrel. Council members tried to get this stopped but supporters objected saying 'It had been fired for twenty-seven years and the show was greatly enjoyed.'

In more recent times ringmaster Norman Barrett had a popular show with performing budgerigars. The birds were trained to play on swings and seesaws. Unlike parrots, budgerigars do not necessarily respond to food rewards to reinforce behaviour and so teaching tricks relies on encouraging their natural behaviours and associating words with actions. He did not clip wings as he found that the majority of birds do not try to fly away once tamed. If birds did get out from time to time they would return to an open cage 'when they get curious about their mates. If you chase them, they won't come.'

Admirers surround a cage of performing canaries for Gicianto Ferrari's act in Llandudno around 1905.

Performing Birds, Llandudno

Pigeon racing and falconry

Pigeon racing could perhaps be considered the ultimate exercise in free flying. The sport involves releasing specially bred and trained pigeons from specific locations. They then race back to their home lofts. Racing pigeons are selectively bred for qualities such as stamina, speed and strength, and for their homing instinct. They are much sleeker-looking birds than the feral pigeons seen in towns and cities. The first pigeon races took place over relatively short distances using motor transport but serious, long-distance racing was developed alongside the railway system which allowed for the cheap and efficient transport of baskets of birds to the racepoint.

The Royal Pigeon Racing Association developed from a meeting of 'pigeon keepers' in Leeds in 1896 with the first Annual General Meeting of what was then called the National Homing Union held in February 1897 at The Spread Eagle Hotel in Manchester. The royal family showed a keen interest in pigeons with both the Prince of Wales and Duke of York maintaining teams of birds at the Sandringham estate. The family tradition was maintained by Queen Elizabeth II, who had a loft manager for the Royal Lofts.

Falconry is a very ancient sport which developed as a practical method of hunting before becoming a pursuit for nobility. It was a common activity in many civilisations around the world and is depicted in the art and writings of China, India, the Roman Empire and the Middle East. Possibly the earliest records are from Mongolia, where it was already popular some 1000 years BC. The Khans of the Mongol Empire practised falconry for food and for sport between the military campaigns. In what is now Iraq, falconry was widely practised in 3500 BC in the Al Rafidain region. The Gilgamesh Epic, an ancient Mesopotamian odyssey of 2000 BC, refers to hunting with birds of prey. The earliest written records of falconry in China indicate that it was established practice of the imperial family during the Chu Kingdom around 700 BC.

Falconry is thought to have arrived in Britain around the ninth century AD and was popular before the Norman Conquest. The last Anglo-Saxon King of England, Harold Godwinson, is depicted astride a horse and holding a falcon on the Bayeux Tapestry. *The Book of St Albans*, published in 1486 and probably written by Juliana Berners, the Benedictine prioress of Sopwell Priory, contains essays on hawking, hunting and heraldry. It describes falconry and recommends different birds for people according to their social rank. An eagle was considered appropriate for the emperor, Gyr falcons for kings, and buzzards for barons. Ladies should fly merlins and young men hobbys, while sparrowhawks were more suitable for clergymen. Even while imprisoned, Mary, Queen of Scots was allowed to fly her merlin.

Aviaries for falconry birds are usually enclosed areas rather than full aviaries. Traditional mews generally consist of partitioned spaces designed to keep tethered birds separated with perches for each bird. There is also a weathering yard to allow the birds adequate time outside. The word mews came from French *muer* meaning to change, because falconry birds were put in the mews while they were moulting. Freeloft mews allow the bird to fly within the chamber, and to choose between a number of perches.

The largest falconry club in the UK is the British Falconers' Club with around 900 members. Established in 1927, it is dedicated to the conservation of birds of prey and has been involved in re-introduction of species such as the red kite, the white-tailed sea eagle and the goshawk.

Freedom and responsibility

Giorgio Vasari wrote in *The Lives of the Artists* (1550) that Leonardo da Vinci, when passing places in Florence where birds were sold, would take the birds 'with his own hand out of their cages and having paid for them what was asked, he let them fly away into the air, restoring them to their lost liberty.' In revolutionary France the idea of liberty was all-important and many Parisians opened the cages of pet songbirds and encouraged them to fly to freedom. Unfortunately liberty is not necessarily the best thing for a bird used to life in a cage and it is said that the streets of Paris were strewn with the dead bodies of canaries. In his *History of*

Lady Murasaki Sets a Bird Free from a Cage, Yashima Gakutei, nineteenth century. (The Metropolitan Museum of Art, New York)

the Paris Commune of 1871, the French journalist Prosper-Olivier Lissagaray reported on the myriads of flesh-flies that flew up from the putrefied corpses of around 20,000 insurrectionists killed and the streets full of dead birds.

In the United Kingdom birds are covered under the Animal Welfare Act 2006 (England and Wales) or the Animal Health and Welfare (Scotland) Act 2006 or The Welfare of Animals Act (Northern Ireland) 2011. These Acts all state that owners have a duty of care and must provide for the five welfare needs of their birds: are freedom from hunger and thirst; freedom from discomfort; freedom from pain, injury and disease; freedom from fear and distress; and freedom to express normal behaviour. It is illegal to keep any bird, excluding poultry, in a cage which is not of sufficient size to permit the bird to stretch its wings freely. Exceptions to this are if the bird is undergoing veterinary treatment, or is being transported or exhibited. In the latter case, the time the bird is confined should not exceed a total of seventy-two hours.

Native birds can be legally kept in captivity if they have been bred in captivity from lawfully captive parents, but the responsibility rests with the owner to prove this if challenged. Some species listed on Schedule 4 of the Act have to be ringed and registered with Defra.

It is illegal to release non-native species or allow them to escape into the wild but many exotic bird species have been deliberately introduced to Britain in the past, either for sport or general interest and others have escaped from captivity. Many die off in adverse weather but some have established themselves as breeding species. The common pheasant, first introduced in Roman times, and the Canada goose, introduced in the seventeenth century, have now spread throughout the country. Wild-living ring-necked parakeets have been known since the 1960s and the species is now widespread particularly in south-east England with flocks of several thousand gathering to roost at favoured sites. Many people love the colour and excitement that they add to parks and gardens but there are concerns of how they may affect native birds such as woodpeckers, and of their impact on fruit-growers.

The beautiful mandarin duck is native to the Far East, but has escaped from captivity in the UK and now breeds here.

The South American Orinoco goose (*Neochen jubata*) is one of the few goose species that utilize hollow trees for nesting. They will readily use nest boxes in captivity.

Treasuring Diversity

Selective breeding

Even bird lovers can be somewhat dismissive of pigeons, especially the rock dove or common pigeon (*Columba livia*), that successful and familiar scavenger of gardens and cities. Pigeons are often castigated for leaving a mess on buildings and statues but they are fascinating creatures with an association with man that may go back at least 10,000 years. Native to western and southern Europe, North Africa, and South Asia, they were the first birds domesticated, before even the chicken and are mentioned on Mesopotamian cuneiform tablets more than 5,000 years old. In Egypt they were reared for food and for religious events. Egyptian hieroglyphics record that Rameses III sacrificed up to 57,000 pigeons to the god Amun in a single religious ceremony in Thebes. The breeding of pigeons has been a popular activity in India since before the Mogul period with fantail birds being highly prized. European settlers first took pigeons to the United States between 1603 and 1607.

There are perhaps a thousand different breeds of domestic pigeon worldwide. Charles Darwin started to study and breed pigeons in March 1855, setting up a breeding loft at his

Flemish engraver Adriaen Collaert (1570–1600) produced many images of birds including hoopoe and owl and this delightful *Two Birds in a Landscape* featuring a fancy pigeon (*c.* 1598). (Rijksmuseum, Amsterdam)

33

home in the village of Downe, Kent. He kept many different breeds including fantails, pouters and Jacobins. His research led him to advance the idea that, despite the vast differences in appearance, they were all descended from the wild rock dove and that human selection of pigeon breeds was analogous to natural selection in the wild. Darwin expanded on this idea in his book *The Variation of Animals and Plants under Domestication* (1868).

In the Victorian era there were a great number of specialist societies for pigeon fanciers. Darwin himself attended a meeting of the Columbarian Society, near London Bridge, on 29 November 1855. Today the National Pigeon Association is the main governing body for fancy pigeons in Great Britain and caters for over 200 varieties. Many are old British breeds but some were imported from elsewhere and developed here. Birds such as the Jacobin are believed to originate from India but were bred in Britain in the 1500s. Jacobins have an extraordinary cape of feathers that would be the envy of any Hollywood diva. The name Jacobin came about because the plumage looked similar to the hoods worn by Dominican friars, known as Jacobins after the Church of St Jacques in Paris. The Old Dutch Capuchine is another hooded breed that has a well-developed head crest that can extend right around the neck. It was probably introduced to the Netherlands from Asia by Dutch sailors during the 1500s and features in paintings of the Dutch Golden Age. Pigeon breeding remains popular in the Netherlands although many birds were lost during the Second World War when German occupying forces banned pigeon keeping in case the birds were used to take messages to England.

Some breeds such as the German Nun and English Trumpeter are known for their crests while Silesian Swallows have fabulous leg muffs. Breeds such as frill backs and the Chinese owl have beautiful curly feathers. One of the smallest breeds of domestic pigeon is the Valencian Figurita. This Spanish breed is bred in a range of different plumage colours but always has frilled chest feathers. Fantails, as the name implies, have a fan-shaped tail. This usually has thirty to forty feathers compared to the normal twelve to fourteen in most breeds. Fantails are popular in Spain where there is a strong tradition of interest in pigeons, including the eccentric racing pigeon races of Valencia and Murcia, where breeders paint their male birds in

Study of a Pigeon, Willem Hendrik Bik, *c.* 1890. (Rijksmuseum, Amsterdam)

Above: The beauty of fancy pigeons has inspired many artists including the Dutch painter Jean Bernard, who studied at the Stadstekenacademie in Amsterdam. *Dove and a Nest with an Egg*, Jean Bernard (1801). (Rijksmuseum, Amsterdam)

Right: A red saddle fantail pigeon as painted by fancier A.J. Simpson for a series of forty pigeon postcards produced for the magazine *The Feathered World* between 1908 and 1914. They featured 'ideal' specimens of each breed and, on the back, a description of the breed's features and advice about breeding.

bright colours and release them to chase after a lone female. The pigeon that spends most time with her wins. The famous Spanish artist Pablo Picasso had a pigeon cote and even named his daughter Paloma, which means pigeon in Spanish. He was given a white fantail pigeon in 1949 by fellow painter Henri Matisse. A lithograph created by Picasso of this dove was chosen as the emblem for the First International Peace Conference in Paris.

The ability to distend their crop is used by male pigeons as a seduction tool. Pouter pigeons including the Brunner Pouter and Amsterdam Cropper are characterized by a very large, inflatable crop. They have been bred in Europe for at least 400 years. These pigeons are so attractive to birds of the opposite sex that a breed known as the Horseman Thief Pouter was developed with a high sex drive and a strong homing instinct, giving it the ability to entice other pigeons back to its home loft.

English Carrier and Dragoon birds were popular in Victorian times. They have expanded beak wattles as seen in some breeds of chicken. The short-faced breeds are the avian equivalent of pugs and Pekinese dogs. The Budapest Short Faced Tumbler is a rare pigeon breed with an odd, alien-like appearance, bulging eyes and a minuscule beak. It was created by the Hungarian Poltl brothers in the early 1900s. They aimed to raise a high-flying bird of unequalled endurance and achieved this as the birds can cover a distance of around 500 miles (800 km), flying for up to 5 hours without breaks. Unfortunately the very short beak has repercussions and there is a high chick mortality rate as the chicks have a hard time hatching due to difficulties pecking at the eggshell.

Smaller than common pigeons, the diamond dove is a native of Australia and was first bred at the London Zoological Gardens in 1868. They have become one of the most popular of aviary birds as they are easy to keep, healthy birds and in large aviaries get along well with other small birds such as finches. The original wild form has a soft slate grey plumage and wing coverts that are adorned with small white dots which give it the diamond name. It has an orange-red eye ring, which is more pronounced in males than females. Diamond doves in captivity are much closer to their wild relatives than are domesticated pigeons, so there is less variation in form but many colour mutations have been selected. The most common is the silver form but there are all white, dark grey, dark brown, red, yellow and cinnamon-coloured birds. More recent findings include pied birds and the white-rump.

The Luzon bleeding heart dove (*Gallicolumba luzonica*) is native to the Philippines, where it forages along the forest floor. It will exhibit the same behaviour in an aviary.

The budgerigar is a small Australian parakeet that occurs there in flocks of hundreds of thousands or even millions; imagine a starling murmuration but made up of lovely grass-green birds. The budgie occurs in the stories and ceremonies of many Aboriginal nations and was strongly associated with acquiring wisdom. It was first introduced to the UK from Australia by the English ornithologist John Gould and his wife Elizabeth in 1840 and instantly became extremely popular. In 1845 a pair were presented to Queen Victoria. By the late 1850s some 50,000 were being imported each year. The first Australian branch of the Society for the Protection of Birds was formed in Adelaide in 1894 and in 1897 the society made a deputation to the state government arguing for the protection of birds including, 'budgerigars taken to England by the masters of ships ... the birds were often crushed in a small space, where large numbers of them died on the voyage.'

Above: A pair of diamond doves will often nest successfully even in a small cage.

Right: Given some freedom, this diamond dove immediately heads for the nearest food source.

With such large numbers in captivity, various mutations naturally occurred and attracted attention. The first registered captive-bred colour mutations, suffused green, grey-winged green and the lutino, which is clear yellow with no noticeable spots or patterns, occurred in the early 1870s. The beautiful sky-blue mutation is thought to have been first found in Uccle in Belgium between 1878 and 1885, but was not seen in the UK until two were shown at a bird show at the Horticultural Hall, London, in 1910. In the early decades of the 1900s and especially between the First and Second World War, the keeping and breeding of the budgerigar became very popular all around the world. Emperor Hirohito of Japan led a craze among Japanese nobility for giving the birds as betrothal gifts from the grooms' families to their brides-to-be. In 1927 one member of the imperial household paid the then huge sum of £175 for a single blue budgie. Crested birds were found in Australia, a deep blue-mauve occurred in France in 1921 and the first albino specimens were produced in both England and Continental Europe around 1930. Even in recent years new mutations continue to be found with black-faced specimens making their first appearance in the Netherlands in 1992 and birds with a yellow face and a white cap being bred in Australia in 2010.

Another bird associated with John Gould is the Gouldian finch. He first described the species in 1844, naming it the Lady Gouldian Finch after his wife, but this is usually shortened to just Gouldian Finch. Native to the grasslands of Australia, both sexes are rainbow-coloured with red, black or yellow faces and a turquoise band across the back of the head. The male has a purple breast while the female's is mauve. Wild Gouldian finches dramatically decreased in numbers in the twentieth century as a result of habitat modification due to cattle grazing, wildfires, and increasing human developments but they are widely kept as aviary birds. A common mutation is the white-breasted Gouldian, in which the purple chest is replaced by bright white feathers. The blue mutation has all the green feathers replaced by blue feathers. This occurs as the result of an autosomal recessive gene and such birds tend to be less hardy.

The zebra finch is one of the most popular cage and aviary birds in the UK. It is a small, highly sociable species and in its native Australia it usually lives in flocks, often mixed with other species of small birds. The original wild type of zebra finch has grey and chestnut colouring with a prominent black chest bar in males, and a black tear drop marking that starts at the eye and runs down the cheek. Selective breeding has produced over thirty different mutations of zebra finches, including white, the crested, and the grizzle, a variety which first appeared in Australia in 1959 in which birds have white flecks across their plumage, creating a 'salt and pepper' effect. Eumos were first recognized in the Netherlands in the 1960s and are very dark birds with a silky appearance to the wings, which results from the feather barbs not interlocking. This reduces the bird's ability to fly.

The Java sparrow is about the size of a house sparrow but is actually a finch not a sparrow. It is native to Java, Bali and Bawean in Indonesia. It was a serious pest to rice farmers in its native range but has been kept as a domestic animal since the First Ming Dynasty in fourteenth-century China. They were frequently kept in Japan from the seventeenth century and often appear in Japanese paintings. If hand-reared, Java sparrows are easy to tame and can form strong attachments to their owner. They breed well in cages and aviaries and continue to be a popular pet, particularly in Asia. Unfortunately wild birds continue to be taken for the Asian songbird trade, which is contributing to the declining population of the species. Captive-bred Java sparrows show a variety of different colour forms including white, silver/opal, fawn, pastel, cream, and agate. White birds come in both red eye (albino) and dark-eyed versions.

Canaries were probably first brought to mainland Europe from the Canary Islands by Portuguese sailors and they were well known by the fifteenth century. They were being bred for export by farmers on the islands from the 1580s and were kept for their song in the coffee houses of Europe by the eighteenth century. Type canaries are bred for a specific physical traits such as differences in size and posture rather than their song. The Melao de Tenerife is one of the native Spanish races and is renowned for its abundant and silky plumage with curly

Camellia and Java Finch, Utagawa Hiroshige (1840). (The Metropolitan Museum of Art, New York)

Left: Dark-crested Norwich and Dutch frill canaries as illustrated in the Player's Cigarettes card from the 1933 series of fifty aviary and cage birds.

Below: Rows of canaries at the Federation Show in 2007.

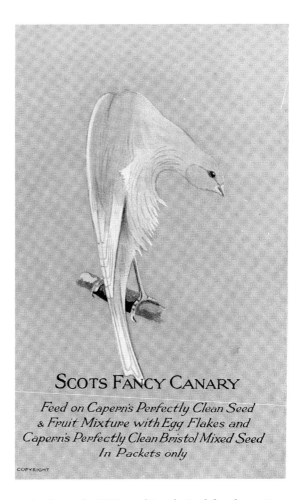

SCOTS FANCY CANARY

Feed on Capern's Perfectly Clean Seed & Fruit Mixture with Egg Flakes and Capern's Perfectly Clean Bristol Mixed Seed In Packets only

COPYRIGHT

The Scots fancy canary, part of a series of cards advertising Caperns bird foods, a company founded by Francis Capern of Weston-super-Mare in 1879.

feathers. The lizard canary arose in France in the early 1700s and is admired for the pattern of its plumage that has been likened to the scales of a lizard, with intricate dark markings set against the rich gold or silver feathers.

The border canary, or border fancy, was developed near the borders of Scotland and England where keeping the birds was a popular hobby with homeworkers such as weavers and shoemakers. It was originally exhibited in Scotland as the 'Common Canary' and in England as the 'Cumberland Fancy'. Modern birds are somewhat bigger than those kept in Victorian times but have the same neat outline and are seen in a range of colours including yellow, buff, green, cinnamon and white. The red factor canary is the result of a 1920s breeding programme by German breeder Dr Hans Duncker involving hybridisation of the wild canary with the Venezuelan black-hooded red siskin. In order to maintain their rich red plumage, red-factor canaries need a diet rich in beta-carotene.

The crest mutation first appeared in canaries around 1770 and the crested canary was highly prized in the 1800s, when it was described as the 'King of the Fancy'. They were originally known as the 'turn-crown'. The crest had a great appeal to breeders and by the middle of the nineteenth century, crested birds were to be found in several breeds including the Norwich and the Lancashire. In the most sought-after types the crest is black and the body nearly clear yellow. Birds bred for their posture include the Scots fancy which was developed in the tenements of Glasgow. It has a tapering body curved in the form of a half-circle from head to tail. The Giboso Espanol is a strange humpbacked breed with a down-pointing head and neck held at an angle of 45–60 degrees.

Exhibition and the show bird

Bird shows have been popular events for hundreds of years with enthusiasts getting together to exhibit their birds and compare them with those of others. Poultry and pigeon shows were held regularly at the Crystal Palace in London from 1857 until 1936, interrupted only by the First World War, and caged bird shows also featured. The *Illustrated Times* of 25 February 1865 has an engraving showing Victorian gentlemen in top hats and women in crinolines enjoying the birds but also the social gathering. Indeed bird keepers of a competitive nature today may relish the chance to win prizes but many established bird fanciers tend to bench their birds as much for the prospect of meeting and talking to fellow exhibitors, as they do reasons of gain. Bird shows can be very social occasions and provide the opportunity of talking to experienced bird keepers and exchanging knowledge that is not readily accessible elsewhere. At the Confederation Ornithologique Mondiale World Show, held at Cesena, Italy, in 2018, there were 32,061 entries from 4,002 exhibitors, representing twenty-eight countries and requiring 138 judges.

Autumn and early winter are the most common times for bird shows when most birds will have gone through their annual moults and be looking their best. Every show will have its rules with birds generally judged on their condition, form, steadiness, clarity of colour and markings, and in the case of hybrids, how well they illustrate their parentage. They should be in perfect plumage. Rarity and difficulty of maintenance may also be taken into account.

Show cages will be much smaller than those the birds are usually kept in. Exhibitors will often attach show cages to their stock cages, to encouraging the young birds to get used to the show cage so they will be more relaxed when the show takes place. Canary show cages are generally of two distinct types. Box cages are oblong boxes, painted to a specific colour to display the bird to advantage, with wire fronts. Birds using these cages include Norwich and Gloster canaries. The second type of show cage is a wire cage used for birds where their position or movement is of importance and include the Belgian and Scots fancy. Many smaller birds such as zebra finches are shown only in matched pairs (a cock and hen of the same colour mutation). They can only be exhibited in the approved standard show cage. Bird shows now are much more carefully regulated with veterinary attendance to ensure that welfare of the birds is paramount but there are still concerns about whether exhibiting birds is stressful to them and shows are condemned by animal rights campaigners.

THE BIRD SHOW AT THE CRYSTAL PALACE ON SATURDAY LAST—SEE NEXT PAGE

The bird show at the Crystal Palace in London in February 1865 attracted members of society to view the 300–400 canaries and a number of other birds including a white jackdaw, a bevy of grey parrots and 'a noble pair of emus'. Image by Harrison Weir from the *Illustrated London News*, 25 February 1865.

Above: Pigeons in traditional open-bottom cages for show purposes only.

Below: A pigeon show at the East of England Showground.

The *Illustrated London News* report on the Crystal Palace Canary and Cage Bird Show of 1883 showed as much attention given to the human visitors as the birds. These included common British species such as wrens and stonechat, as well as the prize-winning crested canary.

Managing a Menagerie

In the year 1110, the King Henry I, son of William the Conqueror, had a 7-mile-long wall built to enclose the royal park of Woodstock. It was designed to protect the growing collection of exotic birds and mammals, started by his father. It would have been a considerable expense in the same year that he was trying to raise the dowry for his eight-year-old daughter's betrothal to the German ruler Henry V. Henry I however was known to be fond of 'the wonders of distant countries' and would beg foreign rulers and dignitaries to send him animals. Henry de la Wade of Stanton Harcourt was given responsibility for the royal falcons and the menagerie that included hyenas, lions, leopards, camels and owls.

The tradition of keeping a menagerie at the Tower of London began in 1204 with King John. His collection is not well documented, although there are reports of him receiving three boatloads of animals from Normandy, and the menagerie included lions and bears. Elizabeth I was probably the first British monarch to open the royal menagerie to the public. During her reign the collection held an eagle as well as lions and porcupine.

In July 1575 Elizabeth made a nineteen-day visit to Kenilworth Castle, owned by Robert Dudley, the Earl of Leicester. He wanted to impress her as he had hopes of becoming her husband and he had a beautiful garden created and laid on entertainments such as hawking and firework displays. The garden featured a substantial aviary built of timber with a

Although undoubtedly beautiful, peafowl can be very noisy. They have a very loud high-pitched meow-like call.

45

The reconstructed
Elizabethan aviary at
Kenilworth Castle.

wire-netted mesh. The top cornices were painted as though they were decorated with precious stones. A recreated version of the Elizabethan garden opened in 2009, based on contemporary descriptions and archaeological evidence. The aviary had to have some modifications to bring it up to modern welfare standards and it is now home to a flock of rare-breed lizard canaries rather than the more exotic species that would have been considered fit for a queen.

James I enjoyed the menagerie at the Tower of London and set up a second one in St James' Park for a collection of exotic birds, particularly those from North America. The pelicans of St James' Park were originally a gift from the Russian ambassador to King Charles II but the tradition continues even today. In 1837 the Ornithological Society of London presented other birds to the park and erected a cottage for a keeper to look after them.

Peacocks were not just admired for their looks but also served roast at Tudor banquets as a high-status dish.

The sulphur-crested cockatoo, like the exotic plant and rich tapestries, is an indication of status in this portrait of Mary Stuart (1662–95), wife of Prince William III, by Caspar Netscher (c. 1683). (Rijksmuseum, Amsterdam)

View of the flower Garden and Aviary

Above: View of the Flower Garden and Aviary at Kew – 1763. Leaf 39 in William Chambers' album of drawings, plans, elevations, sections, and perspective views of gardens and buildings of Kew. (The Metropolitan Museum of Art, New York)

Left: The Menagerie by Melchior d'Hondecoeter (*c.* 1690) is a demonstration of the artist's skill at painting birds and animals rather than an image of a specific menagerie. (Rijksmuseum, Amsterdam)

The gardens at Kew were created for George III's mother Augusta. George II's son, Prince Frederick, originally leased the estate as a family residence around 1730. After Frederick's death in 1751, his wife Augusta, then Dowager Princess, undertook the most significant garden building works. William Chambers was appointed as architectural tutor to George, then Prince of Wales, and went on to design approximately twenty ornamental garden buildings at Kew. The most famous of Chambers' buildings is the Pagoda which is still a much-loved landmark in the gardens but completed in 1760, the year before the Pagoda, was a very impressive aviary and menagerie built to house a variety of exotic birds and waterfowl.

By 1820 when George IV came to the throne the menagerie at the Tower had dwindled but George rebuilt the collection and set up another at Windsor Castle, which was home to many exotic creatures from the expanding British Empire, including emus, ostriches and parrots. In 1828, a secretary bird met an unfortunate end when it put its head into a hyena's cage. George's successor, William IV, did not share his interest in animals and both the Windsor and Tower menageries were closed down. The remaining 150 animals transferred to the care of the newly formed Zoological Society in Regents Park in 1831. The Tower ravens, of course, remain. They have been protected there since Charles II was warned that the crown and the Tower itself would fall if they flew away.

Set up as a competing attraction to the menagerie in the Tower, the Exeter Exchange building on the Strand in London housed a menagerie, run first by Mr Pidcock from around 1773, then on Pidcock's death in about 1810, by Stephani Polito. In 1812, the animals on display, and available to purchase should you so require, included a Bengal tiger, a sloth, monkeys and a hippopotamus, and birds including cassowary, pelican, emus, cranes, and cockatoos. Lord Byron was among the many visitors. The opening of the London Zoological Gardens in 1828 led to a change in the way exotic animals were displayed with more emphasis on their scientific study. In 1829, the Exeter Exchange menagerie closed and the animals were moved to the new Surrey Zoological Gardens. Zoological gardens developed in many cities around this period including the Dublin Zoological Gardens (1831), Liverpool Zoological Gardens (1832), Manchester Zoological Gardens (1838) and Edinburgh Zoological Garden (1839).

Above: Emperor geese are popular in wildfowl collections as they are naturally tame and approachable. They are monogamous birds, the pairs staying close to each other and seeming to chat to each other in a very human manner.

Right: The gardens at Buckingham Palace in London had a resident flock of flamingos until all seven birds were killed by a fox in 1996.

Above left: A Major Mitchell's cockatoo (*Lophochroa leadbeateri*) preening itself to keep its feathers in good condition. Sir Thomas Livingstone Mitchell (1792–1855) was a Scottish surveyor and explorer of south-eastern Australia who greatly admired the species he called the red-top cockatoo.

Above right: The Blue Jan was an inn in eighteenth-century Amsterdam that was known for its small zoo of exotic animals. This image, *Aviary of the Blauw Jan Inn*, by eighteenth-century Dutch painter Isaac de Moucheron shows a magnificent courtyard with cranes strutting around the central aviary. (The Amsterdam City Archives)

Below: *An Aviary*, from *Ackermann's Repository of Arts* by John Buonarotti Papworth (*c.* 1822).

Menageries and aviaries were not new when Henry was busy enclosing Woodstock; many Roman villas of the classical period had had an aviary. In Renaissance Italy aviaries, known as *uccelliera*, were designed by the leading architects of the era and served as focal points in prominent aristocratic gardens. The Vatican complex had one in the Belvedere Villa. The Farnese Gardens created by Cardinal Alessandro Farnese (1520–89) in 1550 on the Palatine Hill in Rome were the first private botanical gardens in Europe. An aviary pavilion had been completed there by 1600, and a second aviary before September 1633. The aviaries were part of a symmetrically designed garden complex that included two fountains. They have been recently restored. The Villa Borghese, just outside the city walls of Rome, had an aviary pavilion designed by Girolamo Rainaldi featuring the heraldic symbols of the Borghese, eagles and dragons. The interior was decorated with frescoes depicting various species of birds. The birds were enclosed with a copper mesh roof. Records from 1616 report that rare and precious birds could be seen by visitors. The Casino della Meridiana is a second aviary at the villa, designed in 1688 by Carlo Rainaldi. Its name derives from the sundial placed at its centre. Between the two aviaries are the secret gardens, where Cardinal Borghese would admire his collection of rare flowers.

In 1594 the English polymath Francis Bacon recommended that a learned gentleman should maintain a library and a garden with a menagerie and aviary. The Georgian estate of Wentworth Woodhouse, near Rotherham in Yorkshire, had a menagerie created in the 1730s by Lord and Lady Malton, later the 1st Earl and Countess of Rockingham. It was a grassy space surrounded by shrubberies and pens mainly for ornamental pheasants from around the world, an interest that developed from the aristocratic love of hunting. The menagerie expanded to include an eagle and a moose, llamas, ring-tailed lemurs and kangaroos. A classically designed bear pit folly was home for a while to an American bear. Visiting in 1768, Arthur Young reported the aviary was a 'light Chinese building of a very pleasing design stocked with Canary and other foreign birds' that were 'kept alive in winter by means of hot walls at the back of the building; the front being an open net-work in compartments'. The greenhouse was home to 'many fine and rare birds' when Princess Victoria visited in 1835 and provided a place for ladies to drink tea. Visitors were impressed by the 'pair of Cockatoos flying at liberty in the gardens'. The aviary was eventually converted into a camellia house but this fell into disrepair and in 2019 was awarded National Heritage Lottery funds to allow for its restoration.

The estate of Bawtry Hall not far from Wentworth was purchased by Pemberton Milnes in 1779. His daughter, Bridget, lived there with her husband Peter Drummond, a son of the then Archbishop of York. The couple had a large circular aviary built for pheasants, particularly the golden pheasant. In 1804 Edward Miller described Bridget's 'elegant menagerie for the reception of curious and rare birds to which she pays great attention.'

The great curassow (*Crax rubra*) is a large pheasant-like species from Central America. Populations in the wild are threatened by habitat loss and hunting.

Originally built in 1805, the aviary and cone house at Woburn Abbey in Bedfordshire were designed by the famous landscape gardener Humphry Repton. The octagonal aviary was divided into a lower section for canaries, peacocks and pheasants and an upper pigeon house. On either side were keepers' apartments, next to the antelope enclosures. Burnt down and disassembled during the Second World War, an illustration of the aviary in *Hortus Woburnensis* showing the original design enabled restoration work to rebuild the aviary in 2011 using green oak. Open-sided cottages on either side of the aviary mimic the former keepers' houses. The aviary is now home to a selection of birds including golden pheasants, budgies and quail.

Renishaw Hall in Derbyshire is a Grade I listed building that has been the home of the Sitwell family since 1625. The gardens are studded with follies and other focal points. The hexagonal Gothic Temple was built in 1808 as a conservatory by Sir Sitwell Sitwell. This was later used as an aviary and even for a time served as cage for a golden eagle.

Orphaned at the age of eleven, William Wyndham Grenville was passionate about human rights and a great opponent of slavery. As Prime Minister he was responsible for the abolition of the slave trade in 1807. He resigned because he refused to agree to the demands of King George III that he should not legislate for votes for Catholics.

Grenville's estate, Dropmore House at Burnham in Buckinghamshire, was built in the 1790s. On his first day after taking possession, he planted two cedar trees and continued to plant at least another 2,500 trees including exotics such as the monkey puzzle. By his death in 1834, the

The Gothic-style aviary at Wick House, Brislington in Gloucestershire.

pinetum had the biggest collection of conifer species in Britain. The flower garden was planted under direction of his wife Anne, who had travelled extensively in Europe with her father and had strong opinions on landscape gardening. Grenville had a great love of animals, particularly his dogs Tippo and Zephyr. The aviary Grenville created at Dropmore is an extraordinary building made of cast-iron with turquoise and green ceramic tiles imported from China around the base and forming the uprights and frieze. Built against a wall, it has three cupolas, the central one being higher than the other two. Inside the aviary cages are four fountains with shellwork basins. Edward Jesse, the naturalist visiting sometime before 1847, reported that it was home to canary birds and silver pheasants. The aviary is Grade I listed but suffered much neglect and has recently undergone restoration.

Now under the care of the National Trust, the Georgian country estate of Osterley Park in west London was described in 1772 by Lady Beauchamp-Proctor as, 'The prettiest place I ever saw, 'tis an absolute retreat, & fill'd with all sorts of curious and scarce Birds and Fowles, among the rest 2 Numidian Cranes that follow like Dogs, and a pair of Chinese teal that have only been seen in England before upon the India paper'.

The menagerie at Osterley Park was home to nearly 100 species of bird, cared for by a 'Menagerie Man' called Jonathan Chipps and his assistant. There is a detailed record of the birds there because the illustrator William Hayes was commissioned by Robert and Sarah Child, the owners of Osterley, to paint the birds for a series of pictures that were later hung at the menagerie. Hayes published 100 of the paintings in book form. The first edition, *Rare and Curious Birds...in the Menagerie at Osterly Park, London, 1794–99*, was the first published systematic record of a single private collection of live birds.

Above left: Edward Lear's painting of the red-sided eclectus (*Eclectus roratus polychloros*) is as full of life and individuality as his famous illustrations for children, *c.* 1832. (The Metropolitan Museum of Art, New York)

Above right: Eclectus parrots are strongly sexually dimorphic. Male birds are green but the females are mostly bright red and purple/blue.

The artist and poet Edward Lear was born in 1812, the twentieth of twenty-one children. Apart from a year at school when he was eleven, Lear was educated by his sisters Ann and Sarah, both of whom were talented artists. They taught him to record details of the natural world around him. At the age of fifteen, he began work giving private drawing lessons and colouring prints. When the London Zoological Gardens opened in 1828 Lear began sketching there and contributed drawings for a visitors' guide to the zoo. At that time expensive bird books containing hand-coloured engravings were sold by subscription. Lear applied to make drawings of the parrots belonging to the zoo and his book *Illustrations of the Family of Psittacidae or Parrots* appeared in parts between 1830 and 1832. His bird drawings were not just accurate, Lear excelled at capturing the personalities of his subjects. The book was highly regarded but not a financial success, although it led to Lear being commissioned by the Earl of Derby to draw the birds and animals in the menagerie at Knowsley Hall, near Liverpool.

There was an Old Man with a beard, who said, " It is just as I feared !—
Two Owls and a Hen, four Larks and a Wren,
Have all built their nests in my beard !"

Lear's Old Man with a beard rhyme, The British Library.

There was an Old Man who said, " Hush ! I perceive a young bird in this bush !"
When they said—" Is it small ?" He replied—" Not at all !
It is four times as big as the bush !"
80

Lear's Old Man who said 'hush', The British Library.

There was an Old Man with an owl, who continued to bother and howl;
He sate on a rail, and imbibed bitter ale,
Which refreshed that Old Man and his owl.

98

Lear's Old Man with an owl, The British Library.

There was a Young Lady whose bonnet, came untied when the birds sate upon it;
But she said, " I don't care! all the birds in the air
Are welcome to sit on my bonnet !"

5

Lear's Young Lady with a bonnet, The British Library.

There was an Old Man, on whose nose, most birds of the air could repose;
But they all flew away, at the closing of day,
Which relieved that Old Man and his nose.

111

Lear's Old Man with a nose, The British Library.

55

Lear worked at Knowsley for five years producing hundreds of drawings. He was a great favourite of the children whom he entertained with his stories and drawings. These tales led to the wonderful nonsense rhymes and stories for which Lear is famous. Lord Derby took a keen interest in the aviary birds and his notes of 11 June 11 1844 report, 'You will be glad to know that my eight young Orenoco Goslings [*sic*] are all doing well. You will find it figured in Lear's drawing, who was much amused by its manner of swelling out the breast like a Pouter Pigeon, which he has represented.' Knowsley Hall now has a safari park, opened in 1971 by the 18th Earl of Derby, and continues to keep parrots as in Lear's time.

The Rosenau, the childhood home of Queen Victoria's husband Albert and his brother, had an aviary and Albert brought ornamental birds with him to England when he married Victoria in 1840. From 1842 he had the royal aviary at Windsor Home Park remodelled to provide accommodation for a variety of poultry, as well as pigeons, bustards, storks and pheasants and a sitting room for the Queen's use.

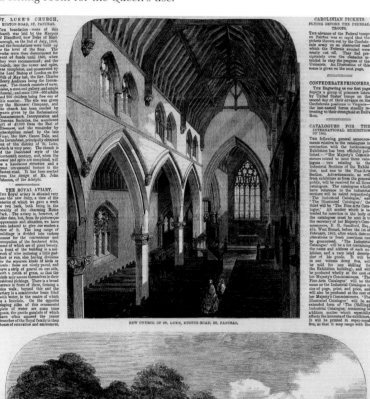

The Royal Aviary at Windsor, as depicted in the *Illustrated London News* in 1861.

The aviary at Monk Fryston Hall was a quaint thatched and ivy-clad building with decorative bargeboards. Cages of birds were hung on the side wall in warm weather.

The Monk Fryston estate in North Yorkshire goes back to the early fourteenth century when it belonged to Selby Abbey. The park and garden were developed in the nineteenth century by the Rev. Benjamin Hemsworth and his wife Constance. They created an Italianate garden, boating lake, woodlands and a maze. The couple used the estate to host social and sporting events including an annual Agricultural Show. These events regularly featured in the local press. A report from 1912, suggested 'The Squire's collection of birds and beasts is worth travelling a long way to see'.

Aviaries and cages lined the paths of the pleasure grounds, housing his numerous exotic birds and animals. There were two main aviary buildings; the larger brick-built aviary had a thatched roof and the ivy-clad side wall was used to hang caged birds to ensure they had spells of fresh air and sunshine. The First World War brought an end to the socialising and staff were conscripted in 1916. In 1923 Benjamin Hemsworth died and his collection of birds and animals was transferred to Temple Newsam, in Leeds.

Sir Morton Peto, the civil engineer, managed the construction firms that built many major buildings and monuments in London, including The Lyceum, Nelson's Column and the new Houses of Parliament. In 1854 during the Crimean War Peto, Betts and Brassey constructed the Grand Crimean Central Railway between Balaklava and Sevastopol to transport supplies to the troops at the front line. He was made Baronet of Somerleyton Hall in Suffolk in recognition

The Victorian Somerleyton Hall in Suffolk is set in a 5,000-acre estate and still has the original ornamental aviaries. The gardens are also home to one of the finest yew hedge mazes in Britain, planted in 1846.

of his wartime services. The aviary at Somerleyton Hall dates to around 1846 and includes a timber-framed octagon with a domed leaded roof and a simple lean-to section with three compartments. The octagonal turret has traditionally been used for native species including turtle doves and yellowhammers but in 2022 is awaiting repair and restocking. The lean-to section currently houses budgerigars, cockatiel and zebra finches.

Lean-to aviaries can also be seen at the Elsham Hall walled garden in north Lincolnshire. This Grade II listed, seventeenth-century country house has an elegant nineteenth-century orangery but the aviaries are of modern design. They are home to a range of birds including Nanday conures, quail, budgerigars and cockatiels and are watched over by free-ranging guinea fowl and peacocks.

The modern aviaries in the walled garden at Elsham Hall are a striking feature of the garden.

Guinea fowl are native to western Africa but have long been domesticated and were present in Greece by the fifth century BC.

The wealthy Rothschild family owned many estates all over Europe in the nineteenth century and these often had aviaries as part of the tradition for owning exotic birds and animals as a display of power and wealth. Waddesdon Manor in Bedfordshire was built by Baron Ferdinand de Rothschild between 1874 and 1885 to display his art collection of arts and to entertain his fashionable friends. Waddesdon's aviary, erected in 1889, must be one of the most ornate such structures in the UK. It has a crescent shape with three separate pavilions and was constructed from cast iron, metal lattice and wire mesh. Its design is similar in style to the trelliswork pavilions in the gardens of Versailles. It was though not just a fashion statement or an exercise in colonial appropriation, the baron was particularly fond of his birds, concerned about their welfare and enjoyed feeding them treats. The *Westminster Gazette* reported that the birds came in response to his whistle, 'They all knew him, and great was the commotion when his spare delicate figure was seen approaching.'

The Rothschild mynah from Bali, a beautiful white plumaged bird with a blue eye mask, was named for Walter, the second Lord Rothschild, a keen zoologist and eccentric who trained four zebra to pull his carriage. The Waddesdon aviary continues in use today and takes part in several conservation breeding projects of endangered species, including that involving the Rothschild's mynahs. In 2011, four females bred at Waddesdon were sent to Bali to improve the gene pool there. The aviary is a listed building and uses modern technologies to provide for the needs of its occupants while protecting the integrity of the historic structure. Three radio-controlled blinds made from special glass fibre cored fabrics are used for shading purposes. It remains a popular attraction for visitors who cannot fail to be enchanted by such delights as the blue crowned laughing thrush and the Asian fairy blue bird.

Above, opposite and overleaf: The spectacular cast-iron aviaries at Waddesdon Manor in Bedfordshire were erected in 1889 for Baron Ferdinand Rothschild. They continue to be used today although the focus is now more on conservation of rare species.

A Walk in the Park

Many people have fond memories of visiting the aviaries and bird collections that were popular attractions in a number of public parks. Often created by Victorian benefactors in the hope of stimulating an interest in the natural world, archival memories of childhood visits sometimes record instead the pleasures of teaching parrots to swear. **Derby Arboretum** was Britain's first public park. It was funded for the benefit of the citizens of Derby by the philanthropist Joseph Strutt (1765–1844). His wealth came from the family silk and cotton mill on the Morledge in Derby. Strutt wanted a botanic garden with trees to provide a place of fresh air and refuge for the industrial workers of the area, within walking distance of the centre of Derby. He hoped, in the less than tactful language of the time, to 'reform the working classes from their brutish

The aviary in the arboretum at Derby attracted families, although a low hooped fence kept viewers at a distance.

and debasing pleasures to an appreciation of the arts and nature.' With this aim in mind, Strutt regularly opened his own mansion and gardens at Thorntree House to Derby's inhabitants at weekends and on public holidays.

John Claudius Loudon, a well-known Scottish landscape gardener, adapted Strutt's plans to include mounds and winding paths giving a feeling of space to the park. Work on the park started in July 1839 and the deeds were handed over to Derby Town Council on 16 September 1840. The gates opened to the public the next day and the Council declared a three-day public holiday to celebrate. Around 25,000 people attended the opening events which included volleys of canon and a fanfare of trumpets, hot-air balloons, a firework display and on the final day, a Grand Ball.

The park originally charged a small admission fee to pay for upkeep but entry was free on Wednesday and Sunday afternoons to allow working people to use the park on their days off. Two Tudor-style lodges housed the gardening staff and pavilions provided shelter for visitors to eat their picnics. A fountain was constructed in 1846 and in 1852, an orangery and entrance building. The aviary and a bandstand were added in the 1890s. The bandstand was destroyed by a direct bomb hit during the Second World War but the aviary remained until dismantled in the 1960s. Many visitors came from outside Derby including, in 1850, Frederick Law Olmsted, the designer of Central Park in New York

Another place that Olmsted visited on his trip to England was the **Botanical Gardens in Birmingham.** Like those of the Derby Arboretum the gardens were designed by Loudon. Funded by the Birmingham Botanical and Horticultural Society, they opened in June 1832. Loudon had proposed a dramatic circular glasshouse, but financial constraints resulted in a simpler range. Annual shows of flowers and produce were held from 1833. In 1910, animals including monkeys, wallabies and bears were acquired to encourage visitors. These were not kept up but the bird collection remained a feature. The current aviary is a more recent addition, constructed in 1995 it houses birds including Quaker parakeets, blue and gold macaws, love birds and softbills such as the white-cheeked touraco in four separate flights. Peafowl roam freely around the gardens and pose obligingly for wedding parties.

A peacock showing off at Birmingham Botanical Gardens.

Right: Aviaries at Birmingham Botanical Gardens.

Below: The aviaries at Birmingham Botanical Gardens look Victorian but in fact are modern creations.

The area of **Cannon Hill** in Birmingham is so-called as it was a possible resting point of Royalist troops on their way to the Battle of Naseby in June 1645. The property was part of the estates of Miss Louisa Ann Ryland. In April 1873 Miss Ryland presented 57 acres at Cannon Hill to Birmingham Corporation along with funds for draining the site, and laying it out as a public park. The park was designed by John Gibson (1815–75) who had trained under Joseph Paxton at Chatsworth, Derbyshire. An estimated 15,000 people attended when the park was opened to the public in September 1873. Ryland had declined the suggestion that the park should be named after her but she did attend the opening. Visitors were handed a card expressing the hope that 'the Park may prove a source of healthful recreation to the people of Birmingham, and that they will aid in the protection and preservation of what is now their property'.

The aviary at Cannon Hill Park, Birmingham, pre-1906, with pheasants and other birds attracting attention.

The park included a carriage drive, two lakes, a bathing pool, shrubberies and flowerbeds, a refreshment pavilion, and glasshouses erected at the Corporation's expense. The aviary stood at the far end of the boating lake and was hexagonal and surmounted by a dovecote. It survived until the late 1950s. Although the original aviary is no more, the Birmingham Wildlife Conservation Park now on site has birds such as cranes and ibis, and energetic visitors can take a trip out on the boating lake in a swan-shaped pedal boat.

The **Arboretum in Nottingham** was the first designated public park in the city. The botanist Samuel Curtis was responsible for the design of the park, which officially opened on 11 May 1852 to a crowd of 30,000 people. In 1889 the Public Parks Committee agreed to pay £100 for the erection of an aviary. Built in 1892 the Grade II listed circular aviary has cast-iron uprights and roof struts. It was stocked with a mix of exotic birds, many of which were donated by local bird keepers. To the north, the brick upper aviary was built in 1934 to house tropical birds. The main aviary is a rectangular brick-built construction dating to the 1950s. The most famous aviary resident was a long-lived sulphur-crested cockatoo named Cocky, whose extensive vocabulary included many swear words. The aviaries face the fountain and lake, which had a variety of wildfowl, including black swans that some visitors were wary of, as they could be aggressive.

Liverpool's Grade II listed **Newsham Park** opened to the public in 1868 in response to demands for public parks to provide Liverpool with attractive open spaces specifically for the working class. It was designed by Edward Kemp, a prominent local landscape architect and pupil of Joseph Paxton. The large lake is the main ornamental feature 'as water is always pleasing'. The aviary was added in 1902, to extend the appeal of the eastern section of the park. The resident birds included a collection of parrots, which were particularly popular with children. The Newsham aviary was dismantled in the 1930s and the birds relocated to Sefton Park.

Stanley Park in Anfield to the north-east of Liverpool city centre opened in 1870. Like Newsham, it was designed by Edward Kemp and enhanced by pavilions, bridges and a bandstand designed by E.R. Robson. The Gladstone Conservatory was gifted to the park by

Alderman Henry Yates Thompson in 1900. The aviary there was a large hexagonal building surmounted by a dovecote. It was surrounded by semi-circular flowerbeds and a low iron railing to prevent the public getting too close and scaring the birds.

Sefton Park, about 3 miles south of Newsham, first opened its gates in 1872, as the third of Liverpool's great Victorian parks. The park was created on land purchased from the Earl of Sefton. A donation of £10,000 from Henry Yates Thompson, a gift to the people of Liverpool,

Above and below: Two views of the aviary in Nottingham Arboretum in Edwardian times.

Left: The Australian black swan is popular in wildfowl collections across the world. Winston Churchill was devoted to his and designed the ponds at Chartwell in Kent, where black swans are still kept today.

Below: Newsham Park aviary in Liverpool around 1907.

NEWSHAM PARK   The Aviary.

The African comb duck breeds well in captivity.

Flower Gardens and Aviary, Stanley Park, Liverpool.

Above: The hexagonal aviary at Stanley Park was part of a carefully tended display in the flower gardens where visitors were requested to keep off the grass and were kept at a distance from the birds.

Below: A semi-circular sweep of aviaries at Sefton Park in Liverpool around 1919.

AVIARY, SEFTON PARK, LIVERPOOL.

enabled the Parks Committee to build the spectacular glass Palm House. The original design for the park by local architect Lewis Hornblower and the French landscape architect Édouard André included plans for a 'Great Aviary', but this was not built until 1901. The aviary was a curved building with rustic rockwork arches. It was home to many species, including parakeets, budgerigars, African grey and Amazon parrots and was considered one of the most important bird collections in the north of England.

Alexandra Park in Oldham, Greater Manchester was created in response to the Lancashire Cotton Famine of 1861–1865 as an attempt to keep local textile workers employed. Opened by Josiah M. Radcliffe, then Mayor of Oldham, the park was named to commemorate the marriage of Albert, Prince of Wales to Alexandra of Denmark. The ornamental aviary was located on a raised grass mound accessed by stone steps, near to the Refreshment Room. It was a hexagonal structure topped with a dovecote, and weather vane. It was formally opened on 26 May 1908 by Mrs Councillor Lees who donated £50 for the purchase of birds including some peacocks. Councillor Lees, later Dame Sarah Anne Lees, was in 1907 the first female councillor elected

Left: The Alexandrine parakeet (*Psittacula eupatria*) was named for Alexander the Great, who collected many birds from the Punjab region of South Asia.

Below: The peacock (*Pavo cristatus*) is a member of the pheasant family, and the national bird of India. Peacocks have been domesticated in many parts of the world, with the male birds in particular valued for their spectacular plumage.

in Lancashire and was active in campaigning for women's suffrage. Payment was made for the park superintendent to enrol as a member of the Avicultural Society in order to learn about caring for his charges. The aviary suffered from lack of attention during the First World War and in 1921 authorisation was given for it to be demolished.

Andrews East Park in Southampton was created as an open space for the use of the town's inhabitants in return for the loss of common rights in the 1850s. The aviary was instigated by council member Walter Alford. It was a circular aviary on a brick base. It was known for its coin-collecting jackdaw called Grip who took coins passed through the bars of its cage and put them in a container. Funds raised by Grip in this way were donated to Southampton's Children's Hospital. The aviary was closed down and demolished in 1993, despite many protests by local people.

Queen's Park in the centre of Loughborough opened in June 1899 to celebrate Queen Victoria's Diamond Jubilee. The dominant feature of the park is the Carillon Tower, erected as a memorial for those who died during the First World War and to celebrate Loughborough's reputation for bell-making. An aviary opened in 1955. It was divided into three sections to house a selection of birds supplied by the Loughborough Budgerigar and Foreign Bird Society. It was originally located by the lake but was moved to its present position, next to the museum in the 1980s.

Originally owned by Kirkstall Abbey, **Cross Flatts Park** at Beeston in Leeds opened to the public in July 1891. The former manor house served as an orphanage. The park was laid out with walks and flowerbeds, a cast-iron bandstand, ornamental fountain, and aviary. During the Second World War when many of Britain's beaches were fortified and therefore unavailable, people were encouraged to holiday at home and Leeds City Council introduced more attractions in parks, including concerts on the bandstand during summer weekends. However Cross Flatts was badly bombed during war with much of the bombardment landing on the park. 5 miles away at Springhead Park in Rothwell, there is still an aviary that is home to budgerigars,

A gardener hard at work with a besom broom, keeping the paths clear outside the aviary in East Park, Southampton.

Children enjoying the aviary and fountain at Cross Flatts Park in Beeston, Leeds.

lovebirds and cockatiels. In 2017 the UK's first dementia-friendly public garden was opened around the aviary there.

The Manor of Balby-cum-Hexthorpe, more than 600 acres of land to the west of Doncaster, was acquired by Doncaster Corporation back in the 1500s. Limestone was quarried there from around 1568 but in 1902 the corporation allocated £250 for the redevelopment of the land as a

The fountain and aviary at Hexthorpe Dell with formal bedding display and rock garden.

pleasure ground. In 1927 one of the quarries was converted into a landscape feature known as the **Hexthorpe Dell**, designed by W.E. Forth, the Doncaster Estates Surveyor. This featured an artificial river with waterfalls and cascades, ornamental gardens, a new bandstand, a statue of William Shakespeare and the aviary. In 2001, the Dell was awarded Grade II listing. It continues to hold Doncaster's only public bird aviary.

Christopher Godmond Pickering (1842–1920) was the son of a tailor and at age nineteen worked as a fish curer in Kingston upon Hull. During the 1880s he owned a number of sailing smacks but sold these to build up a fleet of steam trawlers. He made his fortune in the fishing industry and used his great wealth for many philanthropic causes. In 1909 Pickering provided land on the west side of Kingston upon Hull to create a public park. The iron railings which surrounded the park were taken down to contribute to the war effort during the First World War but the gates of the park were considered too important to be scrapped and still exist. Pickering was presented with the freedom of the city of Hull in 1920 and his name lives on at the Christopher Pickering Primary School in Burnham Road.

At more than 25 acres **Pickering Park** is the second biggest park in Hull. It is free to enter and is popular for its open green spaces, fishing lake and sensory garden. The original aviaries were stocked by donations from local bird fanciers. Backing onto the aviary was an aquarium which suffered from the reduced staffing and care during the First World War and by 1919 the glass had cracked and leaked. The aviaries have been home to a wide range of birds over the years, from bantam chickens to peacocks, macaws and archangel pigeons which have a particularly lovely metallic sheen to their feathers.

A briefing paper to the Pickering Park Trust in July 2017 reported that the birds had to be moved to East Park 'due to an initial mice infestation' and for a while the aviaries stood empty. Following a £500,000 investment from Hull City Council they were reopened in February 2022 with improved animal welfare and veterinary facilities and an education room. The aviaries have been restocked with the city's cultural links with twin city Freetown in Sierra Leone in mind. Residents now includes African touracos and grey parrots, as well as porcupines, tortoises and meerkats.

The East Park in Kingston upon Hull first opened on 21 June 1887, the day of Queen Victoria's Golden Jubilee. The Parks Committee minutes record, 'A more picturesque locality

Above left: The water bird aviary at Birdworld in Surrey.

Above right: One of the most sought after of parrots, the trapping of birds for the pet trade has had a significant impact on wild populations of the hyacinth macaw.

of that extent it would be impossible find on the East side of the Borough or one more adapted to restore the jaded energies of the artisan or man of business when the labours of the day are ended.' Creating the park had provided 140 much-needed jobs at a time of high unemployment in the city. A recent council-assisted lottery grant has allowed much refurbishment to take place. A new walk-through aviary, built on the site of the outdoor swimming pool was opened by popular singer and TV gardener Kim Wilde in 2006. Part of East Park's Animal Education Centre, this is home to glossy starling, Muscovy ducks, canaries, orange bishop and turaco.

Percy and Katharine Stewart purchased **Burnby Hall** at Pocklington in the East Riding of Yorkshire (then called Ivy Hall) in 1904. Major Stewart was an explorer and big game hunter and with his wife travelled extensively, collecting many cultural artefacts housed in the Stewart Museum. In 1935 the Stewarts commissioned waterplant expert Amos Perry to plant fifty varieties of waterlilies in the lakes on their property and this was to become the National Collection of waterlilies which exists today. The Stewarts had no children but left their estate in trust to the people of Pocklington on their deaths. The recently restored Edwardian potting shed is now home to an aviary which contains cockatiels, rosella parakeets, budgerigars, diamond doves, and zebra and Bengalese finches. The garden surrounding the aviary forms the centrepiece of the annual spring Tulip Festival and is then planted up with vibrant bedding plants to provide colour during the summer months. Sadly in 1999 vandals broke in, killing a cockatiel and allowing the other birds to escape.

Pittencrieff Park in Dunfermline is famous for its association with peacocks. The park was gifted to the town in 1902 by Andrew Carnegie the Scottish-American industrialist and philanthropist. The peacocks were introduced to the park in 1905 when Henry Beveridge returned to Dunfermline from India. He wrote of the park, 'And here too is paradise when the citizens of Dunfermline of every age and every class may wander at large and with an open heart … and drink in all the restfulness of time content. And a park without animals is no paradise.' He hoped that by gifting the park its first birds, visitors would find a place of contentment. Images of the park in 1906 show a small wooden aviary and a group of bird cages set among trees. Historically, the peacocks have been allowed to roam freely throughout

View of Pittencrieff Park in Dumfermline pre-1911, when viewing the birds demanded formal attire with hats, as was the custom then.

the park and, if they choose, the town itself. Dunfermline is now home to more than twenty peacocks including Indian Blues, Indian Whites and Black Shouldered varieties under the care of the Peacocks of Pittencrieff Park group. An aviary in the park provides shelter, but they are free to come and go as they please, although there have been concerns about incidents of dogs being allowed to chase the birds.

Ardencraig Gardens in Rothesay on Bute were acquired by the Rothesay Town Council in 1970 and passed into the care of the Argyll and Bute Council. The gardens were designed for the owners of Ardencraig House by the sought-after landscape designer Percy Cane, who had worked for Haile Selassie, the Emperor of Ethiopia, in Addis Ababa. The gardens are famous for the summer bedding displays and have a long timber aviary against one wall that is home to diamond doves, cockatiels, rose-head parakeets, canaries and Senegal parrot.

Lewisvale Park, to the south of Musselburgh, near Edinburgh was presented to the burgh in 1911 by the local Brown family. The stone boundary to the south is the original wall of the Eskgrove Estate. A cricket pitch, tennis courts, pavilion and a bandstand were created for local people to use. A walled garden area was laid out with an aviary on the site of the former greenhouse. The park was extensively restored and improved in the late 1990s with funds from the Urban Parks Programme Heritage Lottery Fund. Birds living in the aviary include budgerigars and canaries. A popular

For aviary security a sturdy padlock on the door is essential.

quaker parrot known as Pollyanna was stolen when someone cut into the wire mesh of the aviary with pliers.

The combined need for security against theft and vandals, modern sensibilities around keeping birds in cages and biosecurity against disease, particularly avian flu makes those responsible for public parks increasingly reluctant to fund aviaries. Perhaps more in keeping with the times is the art installation *Canaries in the Park* created by David Appleyard in 2010 for Whitefield Park in Stanley Road, Bury, Greater Manchester. Appleyard designed 121 canaries to commemorate the then 121 years of the park's existence. The canary theme was chosen because the park once housed an aviary. The canaries are made of iron with a vitreous enamel covering in different colours to represent the colours of the sweets once produced by Hall's Confectionery Works, which stood opposite the park but was destroyed by fire in the 1960s.

The Aviary as Therapy

The histories of messenger pigeons and of the coal miner's canary demonstrate that birds can save lives but birds can also enhance lives and make lives feel worth living.

The golden age of bird keeping was in Victorian and Edwardian times, when all sorts of new and exotic species of birds were being introduced to this country. It was a time of huge interest in the natural world and those people who could afford to do so made collections of geological specimens, plants, birds and animals. Aviaries were commonplace in the gardens of the landed gentry but interest in birds was widespread among all sectors of society.

In Bournemouth the pine-shaded avenue formerly known as 'invalid's walk' provided warm sheltered promenades for visitors who had travelled south to enjoy Bournemouth's milder

PINE WALK AND AVIARY, BOURNEMOUTH.

Pine walk in Bournemouth, formerly known as the 'invalid's walk', had a long run of aviaries with a thatched roof.

climate. The 1896 *Bright's Guide to Bournemouth* extolled the antiseptic properties of the volatile substances, which the pines exhale, and how the fallen needles offer protection from damp. It suggested that 'in Winter, invalids who in other towns would fear to leave their rooms may be found leisurely strolling along the dry carpet.' To keep those leisurely strollers amused an aviary was installed which has recently been reinvented as a domed structure, giving the birds much more flight space.

One of the great philanthropists of the Victorian era, Sir William Purdie Treloar (1843–1923), who was Lord Mayor of the City of London, recognised that aviaries of birds could benefit some of the less fortunate members of society. He wanted to do something to help children with physical disabilities in London and in 1907 set up a trust to build a hospital and college for the treatment of children suffering from tubercular disease of the limbs. The trust acquired the former Princess Louise Military Hospital at Chawton near Alton in Hampshire and established what was called the Lord Mayor Treloar Cripples' Home and College there.

Fresh air and sunlight were thought to be extremely important for good health and great care was taken over the children's diet to ensure they had the nutrition required to help with recovery and growth. In 1916 £160 a month was spent on meat for the children and 60 gallons of milk were consumed daily. The development of physical abilities was encouraged through active play, including the delightful sounding treacle bun race during which the boys, some on crutches, raced towards a line of treacle buns suspended on string from a wooden beam. This caused great excitement as they jumped to bite pieces from the buns. The children were helped to become productive members of society and financially independent. They were taught skills such as making leather bags and surgical boots, so they could earn their own living. The home was considered a model of its kind and visitors came from around the world to admire the facilities which included a workshop and an open-air school set in 5 acres of woodland within the estate, built on the lines of the Forest School at Charlottenburg, near Berlin, a precursor of today's fashionable forest schools.

Treloar's first report to the Queen Alexandra League described the large aviary that had been built on the top of the hill, on the western side of the estate. The aviary was an impressive

Children and their nurse enjoying a visit to the aviary at the Lord Mayor Treloar Hospital in Alton.

structure with arched roofs and ornamental finials. There was a large pond for water birds. Treloar had presented a parrot to the college but this was kept at the home where it was cared for with great pride by one of the boys. The aviary itself was stocked with British birds, most of which would have been local to the district. Treloar hoped, in the language of the day, that the aviary 'may be the means of awakening the minds of the children, transposed in the majority of cases from mean streets and sordid courts, to a knowledge of natural history. It is already a source of intense delight - they love to visit the aviary and watch the birds.'

Funding for extravagant aviaries is of course not available as part of our health service today, even though the therapeutic benefits of bird keeping are still recognised. Several studies looking at the effects of providing aviaries in care homes have demonstrated that watching and interacting with the birds has a distinctly therapeutic effect on elderly residents, promoting a sense of well-being and encouraging increased social interaction between the residents. Residents have reported reductions in depression and improved quality of life after caring for a canary for three months. In the United States, a large aviary containing twenty songbirds of ten different breeds set up in the activity room of a veterans' hospital was found to be effective in reducing depression in elderly males. The mere presence of the aviary had no significant effect, rather it was the intensity of use that produced an enhanced mood, including watching the birds, talking to the birds and talking with others about them. This study in an American veterans' hospital is not a new idea. Images survive of an aviary set among the meticulously landscaped grounds at the Pacific Branch of the National Home for Disabled Veteran Soldiers that was established in the Sawtelle district of Los Angeles in 1888. For thousands of veterans who had physical and mental disabilities, the facility was their home for many decades and the aviary would have been of great recreational benefit.

Spending time with birds may result in the release of oxytocin in the brain. This is a neurotransmitter linked to bonding and affection that has physiological benefits including a slowing of heart rate, lowered blood pressure and reduced production of the stress hormone cortisol. It is thought to enhance a feeling of safety. Interestingly staff members also report that the presence of birds in care homes can encourage friends and family to stay for longer visits.

Residents on a sunny day at the Pacific Branch Soldiers' home. The aviary to the rear of the image is surrounded by trees including a large palm.

Some staff may be concerned that having pets in the care environment will create additional work. However, this may actually provide opportunities for those residents who are mobile to become part of providing pet care and may enhance their sense of worth. Even helping to clean a cage or refilling food supplies can give someone a sense of purpose. It is important though to consider the birds' welfare. They may need a care plan devised as they have their own needs such as food requirements, preferred routines, rest times and vet appointments.

The Uribarren Abaroa Foundation near Guernica in northern Spain, is a non-profit institution that dates back to 1869. In 2017 they launched a pioneer programme based on the therapeutic use of birds, focusing on the care of elderly people. The residence has a private collection of exotic birds with more than fifty individuals of twenty-eight different species, all of which were bred in captivity, and many are unwanted, donated pets. Sessions are held in the occupational therapy rooms giving residents the opportunity to pick up, pet and interact with trained birds. The sessions are fun and assist in motivating residents to involve themselves in more physical and social activities.

Care in the community

Dogs have a long history of being used as 'service animals' to assist people with disabilities and through schemes such as the Pets As Therapy (PAT) charity, which provides a free community service to hospitals, hospices, care and nursing homes and special needs schools. Volunteers visit with their temperament assessed dogs and cats to engage with the sick or long-term residents. Concerns regarding avian influenza limit the use of birds in such situations, however, birds such as parrots are also used as service animals, albeit with a somewhat different approach. With their renowned abilities to mimic the human voice and acquire phrases to use, parrots are able to provide a calming influence over those suffering from various levels of anxieties. A qualified animal-assisted therapist in the south-west of England uses her birds of prey to help people undergoing rehabilitation from surgery improve their motor skills and posture through holding the birds. She finds that young people with disabilities can gain self-confidence and patience while holding and flying the birds. With hyper-sensitive children, being close to birds of prey may produce calmness and can give them a sense of responsibility.

People with autism may exhibit reduced levels of eye contact and mimicry, which negatively affects how others perceive them, leading to the dehumanising idea that autistic people are less loving, compassionate and invested in emotions due to their social differences. However research suggests that they may only appear socially uninterested but actually share the same social needs as others. Although people with autism are less likely to own pets and report lower quality of life overall than neurotypical people, they had higher life satisfaction if they owned a pet. Animals do not judge and interacting with them meant being able to drop the mask that many wore in the presence of other people. People with autism in the study were just as conscious of animal rights as others and working with animals in the community gave them a feeling of accomplishment. Several participants suggested developing a community program in which autistic people could be mentored on pet ownership and perhaps financially supported in the adoption of animals from animal shelters. This would provide autistic adults with the opportunity to own a pet while also assisting them with animal care costs. A pet mentor would be able to monitor the wellbeing of both owner and pet and give guidance on how to care for the animal.

Many people living with dementia and Alzheimer's disease find it difficult to communicate with other people but can respond well to animals or birds. Birds can have a calming effect as they are non-judgemental and not critical. Their presence can help reduce the effects of dementia such as anxiety, agitation, irritability, depression, and loneliness. Having birds around may stimulate memories of previous encounters with pets among people with dementia and can evoke feelings of playfulness and caring, and may help to alleviate boredom.

A black-headed
caique enjoys
freedom to fly at
Tropical Birdland
in Desford.

Serenity Park Parrot Sanctuary in Los Angeles assists with military veterans suffering from post-traumatic stress disorder. The majority of the parrots there are abandoned and often traumatized former pets that had outlived their owners or survived neglect. Many exhibit behaviours such as rocking and screaming, or self-plucking which resemble classic symptoms of the same form of complex post-traumatic stress disorder afflicting the patients in the Veterans Administration Medical Center. The work-therapy programme there, encourages the veterans to bring food and water to the parrots, clean their cages and develop a bond with an animal, which can help people develop a better sense of self-worth and trust, stabilize their emotions, and improve their communication, and socialization skills.

In the UK over half of all people aged seventy-five and over live alone. According to Age UK, more than a million older people say they go over a month without speaking to a friend, neighbour or family member. Such high degrees of social isolation can lead to depression and a serious decline in physical health and wellbeing. Birds are often underestimated for their capacity to provide companionship for the elderly. Birds such as budgerigars can be a good option. They are intelligent birds that are easily hand-tamed and can be trained to return to their cage after free flying indoors. Some will also learn to talk, which reinforces the social aspects. Their cages can be kept on holders at shoulder or chair height for ease of cleaning and feeding and so the bird is at eye level and close enough to enable meaningful interactions. Support of course would be needed to help with the welfare of owner and pet and to ease any concerns about what should happen to the bird if they outlived their owner.

A British Pathé news item back in 1967 on the popularity of budgerigars, discussed how breeders may pay as much as £1,000 for a prize bird but most birds then cost around 30 schillings, although it suggested they should be made available on the National Health. Cages of budgerigars were shown bringing comfort to lonely children at Kingston Hospital and Great Ormond Street Hospital in London and elderly residents in care homes demonstrated the joy they obtained from snuggling up to a tame bird.

Rehabilitation and Conservation

The aviary as refuge

Bird rescue centres in the United Kingdom, such as the Gower Bird Hospital at Pennard on the Gower Peninsula in Wales and the East Winch Wildlife Centre run by the RSPCA in Norfolk, have a vital role in the care of sick, injured and orphaned birds. The Mousehole Bird Hospital in Cornwall was one of the first such facilities in the UK. It was founded in 1928 by Dorothy and Phyllis Yglesias after they tried to help an injured jackdaw that their younger sister Mary had found in a drainpipe in her garden. Jacko the jackdaw was the first of many thousand birds under the sisters' care. Most of these were released back into the wild, although the hospital had over 100 permanent residents.

Described by Dorothy in her book *Cry of a Bird* (1962), the sanctuary became famous during the Torrey Canyon disaster of 1967, one of the world's most serious oil spills, which occurred when the supertanker SS *Torrey Canyon* ran aground off the western coast of Cornwall. Over 8,000 oiled sea birds were admitted for care at the hospital. The RSPCA took over the running of the hospital from 1953 for twenty years, but stopped due to financial difficulties. A public appeal was made and in 1976 the sanctuary became a registered charity funded by voluntary donations. The centre usually treats over 1,000 orphaned or injured wild birds each year. Sadly, in August 2022 the hospital was forced to cull all of its birds when positive cases of avian influenza (HN51) were found on the site and it closed to allow deep cleaning to take place.

The majority of bird rescue centres work with wild birds, but the RSPCA will also look after or help rehome pet birds and deal with cases of cruelty and neglect. It is legal to take in most injured wild birds in order to look after them and release them when they have recovered, although under Schedule 4 of the Wildlife and Countryside Act certain species including osprey, merlin and marsh harriers must be ringed and registered with the government if they are kept in captivity.

Injured birds should be taken to a local vet, RSPCA in England and Wales, SSPCA in Scotland, USPCA in Northern Ireland, or to an independent rescue centre. Experienced bird of prey keepers or raptor rehabilitators can look after injured birds of prey. The Swift Conservation charity keeps a list of specialist carers for swifts and hirundines. Some bird injuries will be due to natural causes such as predators or infections but most problems are caused either directly or indirectly through human activities such as entanglement in fishing nets, flying into windows or getting trapped in chimneys. Birds which have been caught by a cat need urgent attention because they are at high risk of septicaemia.

Wild populations of the ruff (*Philomachus pugnax*) are declining but it will breed in aviaries as here at Pensthorpe in Norfolk.

Once immediate treatment has been given, aviaries are vital for the birds' rehabilitation to allow them to recover and build up their flight strength before being released. Wild birds are easily frightened and need calm surroundings and privacy to aid their recovery. Modern rehabilitation aviaries aim to provide the birds with as natural an environment as possible in order to reduce stress. Plants and shrubs may be grown in the aviaries and food such as mealworms scattered into leaf litter rather than being presented in a dish, so the birds have to forage to find it. At the Gower Bird Hospital staff spend as little time as possible with their patients but they have installed a CCTV system to enable them to observe and assess the birds before release. Videos recorded at the hospital have been used in studies by students from Swansea University to study the bird behaviours and to assist in ongoing changes to aviary design.

Aviculture and its role in conservation of wild species

The island of Mauritius in the Indian Ocean is perhaps best known to bird lovers as the erstwhile home of the dodo. This heavyweight relative of the pigeon was last sighted in 1662, before being hunted to extinction. At least three species of parrot also lived on Mauritius. The large raven parrot survived until around 1673. Thirioux's grey parrot was extinct by the 1760s. The Mauritius or echo parakeet (*Psittacula eques*) however remains. It is endemic to the Mascarene Islands of Mauritius and formerly Réunion. It was critically endangered, having been hunted for food by early visitors to Mauritius and due to the destruction and alteration of its native habitat. Numbers declined throughout the twentieth century, dropping to potentially single figures in the 1980s, when it was referred to as 'the world's rarest parrot'. A number of measures to protect the wild breeding populations were begun in the 1980s and in 1996 a captive breeding programme was initiated at the Gerald Durrell Endemic Wildlife Sanctuary in Western Mauritius.

Wild echo parakeets usually lay clutches of three or four eggs but only one chick generally fledges. Surplus chicks were removed to enable the parents to concentrate on raising those they were left with and to allow chicks to be given to any wild pairs that had failed to hatch their own eggs. Any remaining chicks were taken to the breeding centre where they were aviary reared and then released into the wild. The intensive effort of captive breeding helped to save this parrot from extinction. The species was downgraded from critically endangered to endangered in 2007, and by 2019 the population had reached 750 birds. Other endangered species successfully reared in the sanctuary are the Mauritius kestrel, which in 1974 was the rarest bird in the world with only four surviving wild individuals and two in captivity, and the pink pigeon, a species which outlived the dodo as its flesh is toxic to humans.

Another parrot coming back from the brink is the Spix's macaw, a distinctive species with vivid blue plumage that is native to the dry forests of north-eastern Brazil. It was named for Johann Baptist von Spix, the German naturalist who first described and painted the macaw in 1819. He noted that it was very rare and then promptly shot one, so he could have a specimen mounted. Habitat destruction by overgrazing and collection of birds for the pet trade made a scarce species even rarer. It was officially declared extinct in the wild in 2019, with just a few dozen birds surviving in collections around the world. Export of wildlife from Brazil had been illegal since 1967 but the Brazilian government agreed to grant amnesty to Spix's macaw owners if their birds joined a breeding programme. Most of the remaining birds were closely related with twenty-one being the offspring from a single pair in the Philippines, raising concerns about inbreeding. DNA analysis, careful bird matching and the use of artificial insemination made it easier to produce healthy chicks. Several hundred Spix's macaws have now been bred in captivity. A macaw wildlife refuge was established in the north-eastern state of Bahia in 2018 and in June 2022 the first eight Spix's macaws were released from captivity back into the wild.

The charity BirdLife International's 2022 *State of the World's Birds* report warned that human actions and climate change has decreased populations of 49 per cent of bird species, with one in eight under threat of extinction. This shows a worsening situation when compared to the 2018 report, which found 40 per cent of bird species worldwide in decline. The capercaillie, the largest member of the grouse family, had been hunted into extinction in the UK, but was the first bird species to be deliberately reintroduced, via Swedish birds, back in 1837. Numbers are again declining and in 2022 the scientific advisory committee for NatureScot, the government conservation agency, warned that at the present rate of decline it could become extinct again in the UK within thirty years. The gentle purring call of the turtle dove is one of the most evocative sounds of summer, but this has become increasingly rare in our countryside. The turtle dove has been on the Red List in the UK since 1996. Operation Turtle Dove, an RSPB-led project is working with farmers and landowners to create and protect nesting and feeding habitats.

Alongside these measures, Pensthorpe Conservation Trust in Norfolk have successfully demonstrated how to breed turtle doves in aviaries. They use Barbary doves as foster parents as they are less sensitive to disturbance and respond well to life in captivity. Rearing turtle doves for release into the wild provides a useful insurance policy for British wild birds should numbers decline further, although the RSPB has expressed concerns about breeding turtle doves in captivity, in case aviary rearing diminishes the migratory instinct of caged birds. Another concern with migratory species is that huge conservation efforts in one country are worth little if the bird is not protected along its migratory route. This is being addressed in Malta, where a number of turtle doves were bred in an aviary at Sannat Primary School on the Maltese island of Gozo as part of a project to increase the numbers of these birds on the island. 350 turtle doves were released and eight were fitted with GPS tracking devices to provide information about the movement, flight speed and destination of the birds.

Above: Aviary-raised avocet chick at the Pensthorpe wader aviary.

Below: Avocet family at Pensthorpe.

The Wildfowl and Wetlands Trust (WWT) has been using innovative giant floating, circular aviaries as part of a project to release a group of critically endangered Madagascan pochards into their natural habitat. The aviaries, made using Scottish salmon-farming cage parts, were first trialled at the WWT Slimbridge Wetland Centre in Gloucestershire, using tufted ducks to test that the structures were safe before introducing the pochards. The pochards are trained to feed from the aviaries so that they remain on the comparative safety of Lake Sofia in Madagascar, rather than disappearing into the surrounding countryside where they may be threatened by pollution and human disturbance.

The modern walk-through Waterscapes Aviary at Slimbridge is one of the biggest of its kind in the UK. Designed to allow visitors learn more about native wetland species such as smew, avocets and ruffs, the aviary is beautifully planted with oxeye daisies, campion and ragged robin. The birds are well habituated to humans and so carry on with their normal behaviours in close proximity to visitors.

Modern zoos and wildlife parks usually demonstrate an active interest in conservation and many have aviaries whose inhabitants are involved in scientific breeding programmes. The

Right and overleaf: The Waterscapes aviary at Slimbridge WWT is part of a £6 million project part-funded by National Lottery Heritage Funding to create an immersive and educational wildlife experience at the centre. The aviary structure uses galvanised steel columns and galvanised steel rope, with a polyethylene mesh.

Redshank (*Tringa tetanus*) in the Waterscapes aviary at Slimbridge.

Northern rockhopper penguin, listed as Endangered on the IUCN Red List, occurs mainly in the Tristan da Cunha group of islands in the South Atlantic. Numbers on Tristan da Cunha declined from the hundreds of thousands in the 1870s to around 5,000 pairs by 1955. The Royal Zoological Society of Scotland (RZSS) WildGenes team have been comparing genetic diversity, population structure and migration patterns within different wild subpopulations to improve conservation strategies. Those birds kept at RZSS Edinburgh Zoo act as ambassadors for conservation of this species in the wild and help to inspire the next generation of bird enthusiasts.

Endangered species of birds are protected by The Convention on International Trade in Endangered Species of Wild Fauna and Flora (CITES), which is a trade regulation designed to prevent the excessive and unrestricted international trade in wildlife that threatens the survival of species in the wild. More than 160 countries are now signatories to the agreement including the UK. Birds may be subject to different levels of controls depending on how threatened they are in the wild. Species listed on Appendix I are considered threatened with extinction, and all wild specimens are banned from trade. This appendix includes the Lear's macaw and Bali starling. Appendix II species such as the grey parrot, are those that are considered vulnerable to commercial activities and for whom trade is controlled under a system of permits.

Appendix III species which include many commonly traded African finches and waxbills, have trade regulated by all signatories at the request of one or more countries.

Conserving genetic diversity and historical interest – rare breeds as heritage

There are a large number of rare breeds of domesticated birds which are of significant historical interest for their part in our heritage. Charles Darwin is associated with the eighteen species of Galápagos finches, but his book *The Variation in Animals and Plants under Domestication* drew on birds closer to home, providing an overview of variation, selective breeding and the process of domestication of pigeons, chickens and canaries. All of the pigeon breeds illustrated in his book are still kept by enthusiasts and shown today, although in some cases the characteristics of the breed have become more developed, sometimes to the detriment of the bird's wellbeing. The barb, for example, now has such a short bill that it is unable to feed its own young and chicks have to be hand-reared or given to foster parents. As with the significant ethical problems involved in pedigree dog and cat breeding, the rights and wrongs of maintaining lines of birds that cannot express natural behaviours can cause heated debate.

There are scientific reasons for maintaining rare breeds and conserving genetic diversity. Diverse populations have been shown to be an important tool in medical research. Charles Darwin was fascinated with the beaks of domestic pigeons, which show an incredible variety of shapes and sizes. Researchers at the University of Utah have discovered that a mutation in the ROR2 gene is linked to beak size reduction in breeds such as the barb. Mutations in the same gene also underlie a human disorder called Robinow syndrome, which is characterised by facial features including a broad, prominent forehead and a short, wide nose and mouth. The biologists also found that different versions of a single gene, called NDP (Norrie Disease Protein), demonstrate links between colour patterns in pigeons and vision defects in humans. This association of NDP with pigment variations explains the vision problems pigeon breeders have reported in their least pigmented birds. Part of the NDP gene is important in eye development and the same NDP mutation is also found in two human families in Japan with hereditary blindness. This research could not have happened without the cooperation of the pigeon breeding community in the United States.

In the UK the Rare Breeds Survival Trust (RBST) was founded in 1973 by Joe Henson to preserve native breeds of farm animals and their genetic resources. Through its Poultry

Frillback pigeons have fascinating curly feathers.

Working Group, the RBST promotes knowledge and the keeping of UK rare breeds of poultry including chickens, bantams, ducks, geese and turkeys. The Poultry Working Group includes representatives of the Poultry Club of Great Britain, The Rare Poultry Society, Turkey Club, Goose Club, Domestic Waterfowl Club and the British Waterfowl Association and many individual poultry specialists. The RBST Watchlist includes breeds of chicken that have been identified as priority breeds for support such as the Marsh Daisy, a rare breed originating in Lancashire, the Derbyshire Redcap and the Dorking.

Rare breeds and mutations of cage and aviary birds such as canaries and budgerigars can attract equally devoted supporters aiming to preserve diversity. There are always concerns about inbreeding when only small numbers are kept but interestingly one of the world's rarest parrots is offering reassurance that a restricted gene pool may not necessarily be harmful. The kākāpō is a very charismatic flightless parrot with speckled, rich green feathers, which is endemic to New Zealand. It is thought to be one of the longest living of all birds, with a lifespan of up to 100 years. Heavily hunted by the early Māori people and further threatened by the introduction of predators such as cats and stoats during British colonisation, conservation efforts to save the species began as early as the 1890s. It remains a critically endangered species, with a total adult population of just over 250 birds in 2022, confined to four small islands. Most of the remaining birds descend from a very restricted gene pool. However research has shown that despite 10,000 years of inbreeding, the kākāpō has fewer harmful mutations in its DNA than expected and may actually have lost them over time rather than accumulating them. The results suggest that small populations without much genetic diversity can survive in isolation for hundreds of generations, despite inbreeding.

The Norwich 'strangers'

The Norwich canary is a good example of a bird that has become closely entwined with human history and culture. During the early modern period Norwich, the county town of Norfolk, was England's second city after London, with much of its financial prosperity reliant on the medieval wool trade, but it suffered serious economic hardship in the years after Robert Kett's rebellion against land enclosures in 1549. In 1556 the Mayor of Norwich, Thomas Sotherton, was granted permission by Queen Elizabeth I to invite thirty Flemish families to Norwich in the hope that they would be able to restore the productivity of the city's weaving industry. An influx of Dutch and Flemish refugees also occurred after the arrival of the Spanish Duke of Alva in the Low Countries following the Beeldenstorm (Iconoclastic Fury) of 1566 and the persecution of Dutch Protestants by their Catholic rulers. By the end of the sixteenth century one third of the population of Norwich were Dutch or French speaking. These people were known as the 'Strangers' and were mostly welcomed. Clais van Wervekin wrote to tell his wife that the English were well disposed to the incomers and that if she were to come to Norwich, she would never think of returning to Flanders. Elizabeth visited Norwich in 1578 and the Strangers presented her with a silver cup in gratitude at the welcome extended to those 'frightened by a thousand deaths'.

Many of the immigrants were skilled textile workers and they improved the local weaving industry using new techniques. They had brought with them not just their skills but also souvenirs of home including auricula primulas and their pet canaries. Weavers and other textile workers at the time mostly worked from home in small cottages. Home working allowed them to give their birds attention as needed thorough the day. The repetitive noise of shuttles on loom may have encouraged the canaries to sing and they would have provided interest in the days before radios, keeping the weavers company through their long working hours.

The canary was domesticated in Europe with selections made both for the richness of its song and for its physical appearance. The region of the Harz Mountains of Germany became renowned for the development of especially fine singers, while in the Low Countries breeders

CRESTED NORWICH (BUFF)

Canary & Cage Bird Life.

A buff crested Norwich canary from the Canary and Cage Bird Life series of cards.

concentrated more on birds of various colours including the familiar 'canary yellow' and on a wide range of body types. The original Norwich canaries were smaller and slimmer than those seen today. In the late 1800s the large Lancashire Coppy canary was crossbred with the Norwich to increase its size and colour-feeding was introduced when it was realised that diet could have an impact on feather colour.

In 1873 at the London Ornithological Society's show at the Crystal Palace at Sydenham thirty-five out of the seventy-seven classes were for canaries. The Norwich canary was one of the first breeds to be developed for exhibition. Large numbers of people were keen on exhibition birds and in 1890 a group of 400 breeders and enthusiasts met in Norwich to decided on a new standard for the Norwich breed. It is the bird's shape that is considered of most importance. Referred to as the 'John Bull' of the canary world, the Norwich canary has a rather rounded, robust appearance. Both plainhead and crested forms are valued.

A Norwich canary was selected as a birthday gift for Queen Mary in May 1911 from the people of Norwich. At that time hundreds of working men in the city, chiefly shoemakers, bred the canary to supplement their income. (*Illustrated London News*, 27 May 1911)

Norwich City Football Club was formed on 17 June 1902 and played their first competitive match against Harwich and Parkeston in September that year. Players were originally nicknamed the Citizens, but this was soon changed when the club's chairman, who was a keen breeder of canaries, dubbed his team 'The Canaries' and changed their blue and white strip to yellow and green. A canary badge for the club was first adopted in 1922. The current club badge consists of a canary standing on a football with a stylised version of the city of Norwich arms in the top corner. The Norwich City Community Sports Foundation, a registered charity based at the football club's Carrow Road site aims to support the local community, including disadvantaged and disabled people across Norfolk, through sport. Launched in 2014, their Canary Club offers the chance for disabled children and young people to participate in sports and activities in a friendly, welcoming environment. A clear demonstration of the links between canaries, the city of Norwich and a culture of welcoming strangers.

Further Information

Books and articles

Bugler, Caroline, *The Bird in Art* (Merell Publishers: 2012)

Colombo, G., M.D. Buono, K. Smania, R. Raviola, and D. DeLeo, 'Pet therapy and institutionalized elderly: a study on 144 cognitively unimpaired subjects', *Arch. Gerontol. Geriatr.* 42, 207–216 10.1016/j.archger.2005.06.011 (2006)

Hahn, Daniel, *The Tower Menagerie* (Simon & Schuster: 2003)

Jessen, J., F. Cardiello, and M.M. Baun, 'Avian companionship in alleviation of depression, loneliness, and low morale of older adults in skilled rehabilitation units', *Psychol. Rep.* 78, 339–348 10.2466/pr0.1996.78.1.339 (1996)

Keay, Anna and John Watkins (eds), *The Elizabethan Garden at Kenilworth Castle* (English Heritage: 2013)

Mynott, Jeremy, *Birds in the Ancient World Winged Words* (Oxford University Press: 2018)

Olina, Giovanni Pietro, *Pasta for Nightingales A 17th Century Handbook of Bird-care and Folklore* (Yale University Press: 2018)

Serjeantson, Dale & James Morris, 'Ravens and crows in Iron Age and Roman Britain', *Oxford Journal of Archaeology* 30. 85 - 107. 10.1111/j.1468-0092.2010.00360.x (2011)

Woolfall, S. J., 'History of the 13th Earl of Derby's menagerie and aviary at Knowsley Hall, Liverpool (1806–1851)', *Archives of Natural History*, vol. 17, No. 1 pp. 1-47 (1990)

UK aviaries to visit

Do check before visiting as aviaries may have to restrict visitors at short notice during outbreaks of avian influenza.

Birdworld, Holt Pound Ln, Farnham, GU10 4LD
https://www.birdworld.co.uk/

Birmingham Botanical Garden, Westbourne Road, Edgbaston, Birmingham, B15 3TR
https://www.birminghambotanicalgardens.org.uk/

Elsham Hall and Gardens, Elsham, Brigg, DN20 0QZ
http://www.elshamhall.co.uk/

Harewood Bird Garden, Harewood, Leeds, LS17 9LG
https://harewood.org/explore/bird-garden/

Kenilworth Castle and Elizabethan Garden, Castle Green, Kenilworth, CV8 1NG
https://www.english-heritage.org.uk

Lotherton's Wildlife World, Lotherton Lane, Aberford, Leeds, LS25 3EB
https://museumsandgalleries.leeds.gov.uk/lotherton/

Pensthorpe Conservation Trust, Pensthorpe Rd, Fakenham, Norfolk, NR21 0LN
https://pensthorpe.com/

Sewerby Hall and Gardens, Sewerby, Bridlington, YO15 1ED
https://www.sewerbyhall.co.uk/

Somerleyton Hall, Lovingland, Suffolk, NR32 5QQ
https://www.somerleyton.co.uk/

Tropical Birdland, Lindridge Lane, Desford, LE9 9GN
https://tropicalbirdland.com/

Waddesdon, Aylesbury, HP18 0JH
https://waddesdon.org.uk/

WWT Slimbridge, Bowditch, Slimbridge, Gloucestershire, GL2 7BT
https://www.wwt.org.uk/